# *Making Worк vvorк*

Making Work Work *synthesizes the best thinking in cutting-edge leadership. Scott Hunter explores the outworn beliefs and attitudes that inhibit our growth in relationships, organizations, and society at large. Not only does he expose our stinkin' thinkin'—he also gives us the tools to fix it. A lively, empowering guide.*

> Ken Blanchard, coauthor of *The One Minute Manager*®
> and *The Leadership Pill*™

Making Work Work *should be re-titled —* Making Life Work. *The book presents ideas that will give you profound new insights into how humans think and interact with one another. The principles and concepts presented will also equip you to forge stronger relationships in every facet of your life. Congratulations on a great work.*

> Jeff Silverman, Senior Vice President
> Director of Brand Management, The Morrison Agency

*Scott, I have finished your book. What I really liked and have put into practice and have seen results in are: I have learned to tune out the conversation going on in my head when someone is talking to me and I have found the exchanges to be much more rewarding. I have also started to look for the "gold" in people instead of what do they want now or why are you annoying me. I have also started to look at the world with an abundance mentality as opposed to a scarcity mentality. Your book has caused me to rethink how I interact with those around me. I had a very delightful conversation with my daughter last week and I believe it was because of the tools you have given me.*

> Bryan Volk, Controller, Ryan Companies US, Inc.

Making Work Work *is only the beginning. Scott's insights will help make LIFE and LOVE work, too!*

> Gregory J.P. Godek, author of *1001 Ways To Be Romantic*

*Scott's book is a fantastic road map to not just better relationships but a more fulfilling life experience. The first place I used his road map was at home and my family was the beneficiary of it. Once we started to incorporate his message into our company, people started to report back deeper appreciation for their colleagues. I highly recommend this book to anyone looking to build a great culture in the work place.*

Craig A. Robbins, President, Colliers International

*Scott: I just completed your book, and I think it is fabulous! Extremely well written: clear, well argued, fun to read, great examples, and above all convincing and practical. You really make the case about everyone creating their own paradigm: so why not change it? You also give compelling examples and very practical methods for us to learn to listen better.*

Michael D. Coleman, Ph.D

*Scott-I had an opportunity to read a portion of your book,* Making Work Work *this weekend. . . .I wanted to let you know that so far I find your ideas both intriguing and exciting, as I plan on implementing them to the best of my ability. The idea that I have a choice in "My Truth" about other people and my world is refreshing. It will be exciting to see what impact this has on my relationships not only at work, but in the rest of my life.*

David Beer, CFO, Sun Valley Masonry, Inc.

*Scott understands that the essence of business, not to mention life, is rooted in relationships. Relationships impact all constituencies — employees, customers, vendors, shareholders — and Scott's insights provide wonderful guidance on how to make these "connections" more impactful and productive. I enjoyed the fresh angle he takes, and have recommended the book to many an associate so they can better understand themselves and those around them.*

Michael T. Daley , Executive Vice President
Principal Financial Group

Book 1 in the Making Life Work Series

# Making Work Work

## A Leader's Guide to Creating an Extraordinary Organization

### Scott Hunter

Printed in the United States of America
ISBN: 0-9745111-0-2
Library of Congress Control #: 2003110321

For information about our
coaching, retreats, programs, seminars or workshops, contact

**THE HUNTER PARTNERSHIP ALLIANCE**
Irvine, California
Toll free: 877-237-0207 • Phone: 714-573-8855
Fax: 714-573-8860
Visit our company web site: www.thpalliance.com
or send us an e mail: info@thpalliance.com

For information about booking Scott Hunter as a speaker
Call the numbers above
Or visit our web site: www.makingworkwork.com
Or send Scott an e mail: Scott@makingworkwork.com

Distributed to the trade by
Greenleaf Book Group, LLC.

Hunter Alliance Press

Cover design and layout by Michael Lynch, San Diego, California
Text design and layout by Robert Goodman, Silvercat™, San Diego, California

*I dedicate this book to my friend,
mentor, and inspiration Lew Epstein.*


*Without him, this would
not have been possible.*

# Contents

# Acknowledgements

I AM so profoundly grateful for the inspiration, guidance, coaching, friendship, love and support I have received from the people who have almost magically shown up, one after the other, to guide me on this journey, all of whom have contributed to the coming together of this book. I'd like to use this opportunity to publicly acknowledge them.

Terry Cole-Wittaker, who I heard speak at Santa Ana College in the spring of 1982, and who woke me up to the possibility that there was another path than the one I was on.

Reverend Peggy Bassett, who became my teacher, friend and inspiration for many, many years after I joined her congregation in 1982.

Bob Trask, whose ARAS Training changed my life profoundly and who was responsible for my decision to retire as a lawyer and chart a new course.

Howard Goldman, who taught me the basics of being a business coach.

Werner Erhard, whose work and whose mentorship taught me so much.

Amba Gale, my first personal coach.

John Hanley, for creating the LifeSpring training.

Judith Annette Milburn, in whose Anger Workshop I dropped about 40 years of "baggage" and learned to accept myself just the way I am.

Marlene Clark and Joan Carney, for their friendship and willingness to always be there for me during the '90s.

Greg Godek, author of *1001 Ways to be Romantic,* who signed on as my mentor and taught me about being a published author.

Rita Reneaux, who has been my coach, trainer and friend for so many years and whose endless love and support have allowed me to overcome the many bumps in the road.

Lew and Francine Epstein, whose Men's Club gave me the opportunity to learn about relationships and being related and whose work became the foundation of everything I did in my coaching practice.

Danielle Jackson, who signed on as my coach in the 90's and taught me the meaning of living as a spiritual being.

All of the girlfriends I've had since 1985 who gave me an opportunity to practice what I was learning from Lew and Francine.

All of the clients I've had since 1985 who gave me an opportunity to develop my appreciation of everything discussed in this book. Some of them have played such major roles that they warrant special mention:

Joe Fracassi, President of Pacific World Corporation
Tom Wheat, Esq.
Daniel Cornell, Esq.

Marshall Rutter, Frank Hobbs, Olivia Goodkin, Brian Davidoff, Joel Weinstein, and Curtis Graham of Rutter, Hobbs & Davidoff, Inc.
Herbert Solomon, Esq.
Patricia Lane
Michael Foster, Joseph Konowiecki and all of the partners at The K&R Law Group
John Franklin, President of Sports Source, Inc.
Dan Evans, President of Evans, Inc.
Michael W. Wells, President of REI Real Estate Services

And last, but certainly not least, Stacy Peereboom and Deborah Hinderstein, my daughters, who have loved me unconditionally throughout this journey and ultimately forgave me as I learned to be an appropriate human being and father, and David Peereboom, my son-in-law, for his unending friendship and love of my daughter Stacy.

*Security is mostly a superstition. It does not exist in nature. Nor do the children of men as a whole experience it. Avoiding danger is no safer in the long run than outfight exposure.*

*Life is either a daring adventure or nothing.*

❧ Helen Keller

# Preface

I AWOKE one day in 1977, looked at my life, and clearly did not like what I saw. My marriage of 15 years had finally come to an end; I was separated from my children; and I was in a solo law practice, struggling to keep busy, living from month to month, with not many, if any friends. I had finally come face to face with what I had tried to avoid for a long time: being with me. I clearly didn't have a life that worked.

I questioned what I should do. End it? Settle? Accept my fate? Try to do something about it?

I chose the later course. I decided that there must be something to learn about having a great life that they do not teach you in school. They certainly didn't teach it to me either in engineering school or law school. I committed myself to discovering what that "something" was. And so the journey began.

The events and circumstances that unfolded over the next 26 years were truly miraculous. I could never have imagined them then, and they are truly amazing to me now. I eventually retired as a lawyer in 1984 and began a new career as a business coach. Since then, I have coached hundreds of organizations and tens of thousands of people, and have become a member of the International Coach Federation. I also started speaking publicly in 1984, joined the National Speakers Association, and have since made over 1,000 public presentations. I have participated in so many classes, programs, seminars, and courses that I have lost count.

I frequently say that I have been back in school as a student for the last 26 years. And I have had the opportunity to practice everything I have learned with the thousands of people I have worked with.

This book is the culmination of that journey. It is neither theory nor hypothesis. Everything in this book has been field-tested dozens and dozens of times. My associates in The Hunter Partnership Alliance and I have consistently been able to produce what clients say are "miraculous results," and we have a long track record of creating extraordinary organizations. After receiving a lot of encouragement from others, I finally realized it was time to write this book.

# Introduction

AFTER 17 years of working in and observing organizations of every type and size, I have noticed a common theme among all the successful ones; namely, they consist of a group of enthusiastic, confident, positive people who work together on behalf of a future they have all committed themselves to.

The field of sports abounds with many great examples of what I have observed. For example, when Shaquille O'Neal and Kobe Bryant of the 1999 LA Lakers were fighting with each other, the team could not mount a winning streak. However, as soon as the two star players started to work together, the rest of their team members followed suit, and the Lakers won three straight championships.

In another example, at the end of the 2001-2002 NFL season, the New England Patriots did something I never witnessed in the Super Bowl. Rather than being introduced individually, the Patriots chose to be introduced as a team. At that moment, I knew the heavily favored St. Louis Rams were in trouble, and the Patriots did indeed win.

The early days of NASA provide many more examples. The level of teamwork the astronauts and mission control personnel displayed during the early Mercury and Apollo missions, such as when the Apollo 13 mission experienced a mid-flight explosion, was incredible. Sure, people's lives are on the line so they had better work together as a team, right? But then again, isn't your company's success just as important to you as the success of a NASA mission is to them?

Herein lies the problem. In most organizations, the above observation of what a "successful organization" is simply does not exist. In fact, rarely will you find a group of people being enthusiastic, confident, positive, and working together on behalf of a future they have all committed themselves to.

Why is this? Is it because people don't want to be enthusiastic, confident, and positive? Would they rather be resigned, fearful, and negative? Do people not want to be part of a team? Would they rather be selfish and loners? Of course not.

In my experience of working with hundreds of companies and tens of thousands of individuals, I have found that most people want, more than anything else, to work in an organization where their daily activities nurture them, where they can experience and express their creativity, and where management supports their commitments. In essence, people want to realize their full potential, experience a sense of accomplishment, achieve personal satisfaction, attain their goals and ambitions, and receive recognition and rewards for their contributions.

Unfortunately, the majority of people don't come close to realizing those goals. A recent survey reveals that only six percent of American workers love their jobs. It's a startling statistic, but just look at the culture we live in today. Monday is blue Monday; Wednesday is hump day; then comes TGIF (Thank God It's Friday). People literally "go to work." They trade their life, and a bit of their soul, for a paycheck. They tolerate endless hours of meaningless work so they can have fun on the weekend and during their two-week vacation.

What a sad state of affairs! This mindset not only robs people of the aliveness that's possible at work, but also it robs the company of the productivity and creativity that is possible in a nurturing environment. It doesn't have to be this way, and the power to change this situation is within each of us.

We are living in remarkable times – no one can deny that fact. As we began the 21$^{st}$ Century, technology breakthroughs were occurring daily. Today, I'm not writing this book with a pencil on a tablet. Rather, I'm writing it on a portable computer that I can take with me as I fly at 35,000 feet from one location to another.

Yet, while technology was and still is evolving rapidly, and everyone is jumping on the technology bandwagon, the quality of our interpersonal relations has improved very little, if at all. Personality conflicts, power struggles, unspoken hidden agendas, misunderstandings, people not feeling appreciated or understood, and turnover are everyday occurrences that negatively impact a company's bottom line and rob people of the enthusiasm they yearn for at work.

Do you want a truly "successful organization"? More important, are you committed to developing one? If you want to be as effective with people as you are with technology, and if you want to create the kind of company you hope is possible, then read on. You will discover that there are only a few reasons why the present business climate exists. Together we will look at those reasons, and then we will explore what we can do, as well as what has been done, to overcome the reasons so you can create the organization of your dreams.

*Chapter 1*

# The Power of Paradigms

WE START our discussion by looking at "paradigms." A couple of definitions are useful.

In his book *Powers of the Mind,* Adam Smith defines a "paradigm" as "a shared set of assumptions." What an enlightening definition! An assumption is something we take for granted. And if we have a set of things we take for granted, and we all share that set of things, then we have a paradigm. The fact that people thought the earth was flat in the 1400s is a perfect example. It was a "fact" everyone took for granted, and so it was the dominant paradigm of the day.

Smith continues by saying, "A paradigm is the way we perceive the world; water to the fish. A paradigm explains the world to us and helps us to predict its behavior. When we are in the middle of a paradigm, it is hard to imagine any other paradigm."

Smith's analogy of a paradigm being like "water to the fish" is interesting, because he's suggesting that a fish doesn't know it's swimming in water. In order for a fish to know that there is an environment other than water, it would need to come out of the water. Unless that happens, the fish is as blind to the fact that it is swimming in water as the bird is to the fact that it is flying in the air.

The closing sentence in Smith's definition adds the final touch to our fish/bird analogy. When you are in the middle of a paradigm, and that paradigm is all you know, it's hard to imagine things any other way!

## Another Look

In his book *An Incomplete Guide to the Future,* Willis Harmon defines a paradigm as "the basic way of perceiving, thinking, valuing and doing associated with a particular vision of reality." He further says, "A dominant paradigm is seldom, if ever, stated explicitly; it exists as unquestioned; it is a tacit understanding that is transmitted through culture and to succeeding generations through direct experience rather than being taught."

Harmon is adding to Smith's definition by saying that a paradigm is the way we think given our vision of reality. And because we can't imagine life being any other way, no one questions the paradigm. It just is.

Armed with those definitions, we can appreciate that at any time, and at all times, we live in a paradigm, and many aspects of our current world's paradigm impact our everyday lives. It's important to understand that fact for several reasons. First, a paradigm is invisible; it's transparent; yet it's there as much as the air we breathe. And because our paradigm shapes our thinking, values, and actions, it literally uses our lives. That is to say, the paradigm in which we live tells us what we can and cannot think, what we can and cannot do, and what we will and will not believe.

For example, let's go back to the 15$^{th}$ Century idea that the earth was flat. It's not that people in the 1400s believed the earth was flat; to them, the earth just was flat. It's doubtful that one person said to another, "I believe the earth is flat. What do you believe?" The belief just was. And what don't you do when the earth is flat? Sail close to the edge! So people in those days didn't.

Another example of how our paradigm shapes our thinking is from the early 1950s. Back then, people thought it was impossible for a human being to run a four-minute mile. And what don't you do when something is impossible? Try! Was it impossible? Of course not. But if you think something is impossible, it shapes your actions, whether true or not. So, when Roger Bannister ran a mile in under four minutes, it didn't take long for dozens of others to do the same. Today, this accomplishment is commonplace.

My favorite example of the power of a paradigm comes from the watch manufacturing industry. In 1963, Switzerland manufactured 85% of the world's watches. Five years later, that same country manufactured just 15% of the world's watches, and over 30,000 Swiss workers lost their jobs. What happened? The quartz crystal digital watch came along.

Many people mistakenly think the Japanese invented the digital watch. In reality, it was invented by a group of Swiss engineers. But when the engineers took their invention to the higher-ups in the Swiss watch industry, the executives thought it was just a toy and nothing to take seriously. Why? Because to them, *the new device didn't fit within their paradigm.*

So what happened? That year, like every other year, there was a watch show in Switzerland. People came from all over the world to see the latest watches. The Swiss inventors displayed their "toy" without any thought of what might happen. But when people from Texas Instruments and Seiko saw the "toy," they envisioned much more. They took the proverbial ball and ran with it, and the rest is history. Thirty thousand people lost their jobs and a country lost a big chunk of its industry, all because of the power of a paradigm.

## What Does All This Mean?

A paradigm acts as an information filter so that what we perceive as reality is determined by our paradigm. What may be perfectly obvious to people with one paradigm may be completely invisible to people with a different paradigm.

Finally, and most important, our paradigm determines what we can and cannot accomplish. For example, if you take a piece of land measuring one hundred yards, mark off lines every ten yards, put goal posts at opposite ends, and then give everyone baseball gloves and bats, the people are going to find it difficult to play baseball because the field isn't set up for that.

So it is in life. We live in a particular paradigm. And it's important to understand that. It's neither good nor bad. It just is what it is. But the paradigm you and I are living in has just as much impact on us as the paradigm in the 1400s had on the people who lived then. The current paradigm is causing us to be and act in a particular way. And like water to the fish, we can't even see it!

So neither you nor I is responsible for our world being the way it is. It was that way when we arrived, and we got trained to operate in it just like everyone else did. As we will discuss more fully as we proceed, the existing paradigm, the one right here and now, is not set up to have a group of enthusiastic, confident, positive people working together on behalf of a future they have all committed themselves to. On the contrary, it is set up to have pettiness, gossiping, competition, conflict, arguments, and righteousness. How do I know that? Because that's precisely what we frequently have!

And if we keep operating in the existing paradigm as we have in the past, we'll keep getting more of what we already have. Albert Einstein defined insanity as doing the same thing over and over again, thinking you'll get a different result. So if you stop and think about it, we're all a little insane, aren't we?

There's a funny story that is told about a man walking down a dark street late one evening. As he approaches a lamppost, he sees a second man searching for something on the ground. Not seeing anything, the first man says to the second, "Excuse me, did you lose something?" The second man replies, "Yes, I lost my keys." So the first man joins the search for a bit. Not seeing anything, he says, "I don't see anything. Are you sure you lost them here?" The second man replies, "Actually, no. I think I lost them down the street." A bit bewildered, the first man asks, "Well then, why are you looking here?" The second man answers, "Because this is where the light is!"

The same thing happens in life. We keep looking for what we're looking for in the same places we've always looked, even though we don't find the joy, the aliveness, the fun, and the team spirit we want at work. As John Stuart Mill said, "When society requires to be rebuilt, there is no use in attempting to rebuild it on the old plan. No great improvements in the lot of mankind are possible, until a great change takes place in the fundamental constitution of their modes of thought."

And that's exactly what I'm going to ask you to do as you lead your company into the future. I want you to initiate a great change in the fundamental constitution of your thinking. Anything less will be like putting a bandage on a broken arm. It might look good, but it isn't going to get the job done. So forget the bandage solutions! They don't work. It's time to finally understand that if we stay as we are, we'll only get more of what we've got.

## Embark on a Journey of Change

From here on out, you and I will shine some light on the existing paradigm, take it out of the invisible realm, see it for what it is, and understand how it causes us to act as human beings. This exercise will make it immediately apparent why our companies, and indeed our world, are in the shape they are in. And I hope it will also be apparent that the way we are is only one possible way of being a human being. We will then propose an alternative paradigm – another possible way of being – that will enable us to have cooperation, caring, cohesiveness, trust, respect, and most important for you as a company leader, satisfaction, fulfillment, harmony, creativity and productivity.

Once we do this and commit to this new way of being, everything will begin to flow. Set up the field with a diamond, bases, and a pitcher's mound and it's easy to play baseball. The only thing left to do is practice the new way of being until you get good at it, and that shouldn't take long if you're willing to commit yourself to it.

Sound too good to be true? It isn't . . . as long as you're willing to tell the truth and do the work. And in the final analysis, that may be the biggest challenge of all. As we will discuss more fully in Chapter Two, people don't want to change. They don't want to admit that they don't know everything already. And most people want to be right and blame everyone and everything else for all their problems and failures. But if you're willing to move beyond that, the results can be both extraordinary and amazing.

*The problem in my life and other people's lives is not the absence of knowing what to do but the absence of doing it.*

＊ Peter Drucker


*The important thing is this: to be able at any moment to sacrifice what we are for what we could become.*

＊ Charles DuBois

*Chapter 2*

# The Components of Knowledge

IN TODAY's paradigm, we think, or should I say "assume," that knowledge is divided into two components. The first is "what we know." Knowing information is useful, because we can use what we know to produce results. And I'm sure you do this all of the time.

The second component is "what we know we don't know." And, of course, there are many things we know we don't know. I, for example, know that I don't know much if anything about chemistry, medicine, nuclear science, and biomechanics, to name a few subjects. The recent performance of my stock portfolio tells me I don't know much about investing either.

Fortunately, for the most part, we're good at dealing with what we know we don't know. We find a class, a book, or someone who knows something about what we don't know, and we take the class, read the book, or ask a question so we can take what we don't know and move it into the column of what we do know. We can then use that knowledge to produce results.

If you look at that process, you'll see that it's fundamentally closed ended. In other words, we continue until we are satisfied that we know enough to be able to produce the results we want, and then, most of the time, we stop right there.

But what if there was a third component to knowledge? What if, in addition to "what we know" and "what we know we don't know," there was "what we don't know we don't know"? In this category are all the things we are blind to. They are there, but we can't see them because either we don't know they are there or we don't know to look for them.

For example, when you go outside on a clear, dark night and look up at the sky, what do you see? Most people answer, "stars." Now suppose an astronomer joins you. The two of you spend a couple of evenings looking up at the sky. With the astronomer's guidance, you'll probably be able to pick out some planets, suns, moons, galaxies, and satellites. Next an astrologer joins you and you spend a couple of evenings with him. Now you're able to see Virgo, Capricorn, Libra, and Pisces in those mere stars.

Where were the planets, galaxies, and constellations before your two experts arrived? The answer: they were always there; you simply didn't have the eyes to see them.

## The Great Unknown

Unfortunately, just as in the last example, there is much we can't see even though it's there right under our noses, which is a truly frustrating predicament. After all, if we don't know that something even exists, how can we formulate a question to ask about it? The answer is that we can't.

And by the very nature of the current paradigm, there is much that is invisible. What we want and what we need is there, but we can't see it. And the fact that it's there, using us without our knowledge or understanding, creates the problems we experience, hampers our relationships, and prevents us from effectively leading our teams.

So please realize that your goal here is not to learn more "stuff." I don't doubt the fact that you are already smart. Your goal is to take what lives in the unseen and bring it to the light of day. When you can see what has been hidden from you for so long, you will become more effective in accomplishing what is already in front of you.

Together we will go on a journey and engage in a dialog about things you may not know, as well as things you may not know you do not know. Your job is to go on the journey with me and just look . . . but not for answers. Sure, you may find some answers, but those are the booby prizes. They're not what we're looking for. Instead of looking for answers, we're looking for insights or "a-ha" moments. My objective is to have you see things you haven't seen before.

During our journey, I'm going to continuously ask you to "map it onto your experience." By this, I mean I want you to think about what I just said, reflect on it, and compare it with your own experiences. Discover what fits and what doesn't. Perhaps something I say will explain what you see on a day-to-day basis in doing your job in a way you haven't seen before or in a way that allows you to handle a tough situation more effectively.

My hope is to arouse your curiosity so you keep looking and inquiring into the subjects we'll discuss. No, this book is not "the answer." I'm not smart enough to give you *the* answer. And I'm certainly not smart enough or know enough about you to give you *your* answers. (I find it difficult to formulate my own answers sometimes.) Therefore, the challenge is to give up the need for answers and be happy with the search.

## The Nature of an Inquiry

Here's an example from my own life to show you how the process works. I married right out of college, and for all the wrong reasons. I was leaving home for the first time, and frankly, I was scared to be on my own. So I married someone who would keep me company on my journey into the unknown. Whether we were compatible or even whether we loved each other wasn't relevant; I just didn't want to be alone.

As I am sure you have already guessed, that relationship did not turn out well. Fifteen years and two children later, we divorced. I bummed around and dated for several years, but when it came to relationships, I was as clueless then as I was in college. So in the early '80s, I just gave up. I didn't know how to have a successful relationship, so I stopped trying. "Love 'em and leave 'em" became my mantra.

Then, in 1985, during my first job as a business coach, one of the coaches in the company I joined asked me if I was in a relationship. I quickly gave him my standard answer: "I don't do relationships." I don't recall the exact conversation that ensued, but I do remember he convinced me that my decision to not pursue a relationship was not a useful one, and that it would be a lot wiser for me to learn how to have a great relationship rather than give up.

I remember saying to him, "Okay. I'm going to learn what it takes to have an extraordinary relationship with everyone in my life and with a woman in particular." Thus began the inquiry into "what I needed to know" and "whom I needed to be" to have extraordinary relationships with the people in my life.

No matter how much time passes, that inquiry never ends. Every day is another opportunity for me to discover what I don't know I don't know. And while I've found a few things that look like "answers," and they are frequently useful, the inquiry never seems to stop. I have gotten many insights into the nature of human beings and the nature of relationships. I've had many "a-ha" moments, and I now see many things I couldn't see before.

These insights have allowed me to experience far more satisfying relationships than I ever thought possible. As I've shared these insights with clients, they have been able to achieve similar results.

So don't look for answers here. I don't offer formulas, prescriptions, rules, habits or "ten steps." My job is to take you on a journey into the existing paradigm. Map what you read onto your experience. See if it fits. Try out the ideas. Be open to where they take you and be willing to "try on" what I say.

Dr. Martin Luther King, Jr. once said, "Who we are as human beings is only increasing that which we already know and which we have a reference for. We want a quick fix, an easy answer, the fast solution." Please don't be one of these "quick fix, easy answer, fast solution" people. They never get far anyway.

Relationships will continue to be a challenge and a struggle. But armed with the insights this book offers, you'll be on your way to having rich, meaningful relationships with everyone in your company and in your life as you provide extraordinary leadership for your team.

One last caution: After having this dialog with thousands of people, I have found that many individuals have a difficult time relating to information they don't understand, they have not heard before, or they have no reference for. They respond in a variety of ways. Some get angry, while others get defensive; some get frustrated, others resist, and the rest argue. In extreme cases, they check out. Their body is there, but they are gone.

You may have any or all of these reactions, and that's okay. They're all normal and human. The important thing is that you hang in there. We're building something here, and you won't clearly see the power and value of it until you get close to or arrive at the end. It's like a jigsaw puzzle. The picture doesn't become clear until most, if not all, of the pieces are there. But if you hang in there to the end and don't skip over anything, I promise you the results can be nothing short of miraculous.

## Declare Your Commitment

The value you get out of this book will be directly related to what you're committed to getting out of it. Recall the last time you flew on an airplane. As the plane taxied from the gate, the flight attendant or the TV monitor delivered the pre-flight safety instructions. What were you and most of the other passengers doing at that moment? Most likely it was something other than listening and watching. Hey, you've heard it all before, right? Besides, at that moment, you weren't concerned about anything in particular.

But suppose you are flying at 30,000 feet, and suddenly the plane begins to shake. Out the window you can see smoke coming from one of the engines. Just then, the flight attendant announces that you are going to make an emergency water landing. She proceeds to give you instructions on how to prepare. Do you listen to her now? You bet. Why? Because now something is clearly at stake, namely your life. When something important is at stake, we listen in a different way. Our commitment is different.

I remember an incident that brought this point home clearly to me. In the late '80s, I was part of a company that was exploring the phenomenon of coaching and what it took to coach people to produce extraordinary results. As part of our work, we staged an event with some of the day's greatest sports coaches to learn what we could about what made them great coaches. Those in attendance were Red Auerbach, the Boston Celtics basketball team coach, John Wooden, the basketball coach from UCLA, George Allen, the football coach of the Washington Redskins, and Tim Galway, the author of *The Inner Game of Tennis*.

Our company President interviewed the four coaches in a TV studio, and we broadcast the program around the country. I sold tickets and hosted a viewing in southern California, where we had about 100 people watch the interview. At the end, we had a discussion about what people learned from the conversation.

One man eagerly leaped to his feet and said that he had been in corporate America for over thirty years with many Fortune 500 companies, and that he had participated in innumerable programs. He thought that this was the most powerful, insightful, and valuable program he had ever witnessed. He couldn't wait to get to work so he could put into practice what he had learned.

Then another man stood up. He was a company CEO and a former pro football player. His comments were that it was fun, that Red was a bit of a character, that John was very charismatic, and that George was obviously smart and intense, but that was it.

Then another man, an accountant, stood up and said that this had to be the stupidest program he had ever attended. He claimed that it was a total waste of time, and he wanted his money back, which I gladly gave him as he stormed out the door.

How could three people at the exact same program have such different reactions? Simple. Each came expecting something different, and each had a very different commitment.

So before you continue, please get a pen and fill out the chart on the following page.

At this point you may be wondering what precisely constitutes a "breakthrough." My definition of a breakthrough is an unprecedented or unexpected result, something you cannot predict. It is out of the ordinary, not a reasonable extension of the past. It may be something that others broadly accept as a breakthrough, or something very personal.

Now write!

*The breakthroughs I am committed to producing as a*
*result of my reading this book are . . .*

| Personal | Business |
|---|---|

**Personal**

① Excel in my Job to the point of becoming the best

② Establish a thriving Business that

③ helps people and achieve financial independence

**Business**

① Find a formula to relate to my sons.

② Make a impact on the lives of other fellow Muslims.

③ Take Car of my health to control hypertension, B, and itching

What are you willing to put on the table for exploration as you read this book? What kind of commitment do you have to your business and to your personal life to produce a "breakthrough" as a result of what you will learn from this book? What relationships are not as strong as you'd like them to be? In what areas do you feel inadequate, insufficient, ineffective, or frustrated as a leader? What results do you want to produce that you're not currently producing? What problems do you have that you can't solve?

When I do executive retreats and ask people to do this exercise, they write down remarkable things. Some statements are simple, such as, "I'd like to be able to say what's on my mind without fear of retribution." Others are as heart wrenching as, "I haven't spoken to my brother for thirty years and would like to know what to do about that." So please don't proceed without writing down what's important to you.

The comedian Flip Wilson once said, "What you lose is what you don't bet when you win." Don't make the mistake of not winning *really, really* big because you neglected to bet on what you could accomplish. In writing this book, I committed to provide you the insights necessary for you to be an extraordinary leader, to create an extraordinary organization, and for you and all the people around you to win big. In fact, you can't lose. So you might as well bet the farm. Mention everything that you would like to get out of reading this book. I promise that it's all within your reach.

## Chapter 3

# The "Conversation"

THROUGHOUT THE day, from the moment you wake up to the time you fall asleep, something remarkable takes place. When you're showering, getting dressed, eating breakfast, driving to work, sitting at your desk, participating in a meeting, eating lunch, driving home, cooking dinner, preparing for bed – in other words, all the time – there's a conversation going on. You know the one. It's part of the internal dialog that just asked you, "What conversation is he talking about?" It's the conversation you wake up with in the morning, that's with you all day, and sometimes keeps you up at night.

How do you relate to that conversation? What do you call it? Typical answers I get from audiences are: thinking, having thoughts, self-talk, my mother, the committee, radio Hanoi, the gremlin, and others. What you label the conversation doesn't matter. What matters is that you notice the conversation and realize it's there all the time. And while sometimes you are in control of the conversation, more often you are not.

For example, aren't there times when you are driving in your car, sitting at your desk, flying across country, etc., and you find yourself in the middle of a conversation and you have no idea why? And aren't there times when something is "on your mind" and you wish whatever it is would just go away and leave you alone but it won't?

Unfortunately, most people don't pay much, if any, attention to that conversation. "Why should we?" they ask. "It's just self-talk or thinking." No . . . it's much more than that.

## In The Beginning

Let's first talk about where that conversation comes from – at least my understanding of where that conversation comes from and what it's all about.

When we are born, for all practical purposes, there is no conversation. But it doesn't stay that way for long. All kinds of events occur: our diaper is wet; we're hungry; we hear a loud noise; we're picked up; we need to burp; we cry. Sometimes someone comes to take care of us right away; other times they don't. At any given time, any one of a number of people is around us doing something. Mothers, fathers, sisters, brothers, grandparents . . . the list goes on and on.

Soon we grow, mature, and develop a personality. We crawl; we walk; people react to what we do. We go to school and interact with other children and teachers. The number of events we experience is endless.

In reality, none of these events inherently mean anything. I know you likely don't believe that statement, and that's okay. Human beings have a hard time believing that events don't mean anything. In fact, we believe just the opposite. We think *everything* that happens means *something*.

So, beginning at an early age, we start interpreting everything that occurs and assigning it a meaning. And it's important to understand that for us, the event does indeed have the meaning we give it, whether fact or not. For us, it is "true."

Then we store the event, with the meaning we gave it, in our consciousness. Of course, it doesn't stop there. The next event occurs, we interpret it, give it some meaning, and store it away. We repeat this process again and again and again. Along the way, we make judgments and decisions about ourselves, the world, other people, and how we fit in. What emerges is an elaborate story about everything. The entire process – the decisions, the judgments, the story – are all a part of our conversation.

Therefore, your conversation – the one you wake up to in the morning and the one that stays with you all day and into the night – is the sum total of the process just described. Stored within you are all the events you have ever experienced, with the meaning you gave them attached, and all the decisions, judgments and concepts that evolved as a result of that process.

Later we will discuss some of the judgments and decisions we often make. For now, it is sufficient to say that you live in a conversation, that within that conversation is your paradigm, and that what makes you *you* is that conversation.

**How it Evolves**

Here's something interesting to consider, something I have heard so many times from so many reputable sources, that I believe it is true: If I could listen to your conversation, the one that is using your life and determining who you think you are, who you think other people are, and everything else about the world you live in, I would find that 50% of your conversation today was there by the time you were five years old! I would further find that 80% of your conversation today was there by the time you were eight years old, and 95% of your conversation today was there by the time you were eighteen years old.

Now that's scary. It means that at least 80% of the time, the person doing the thinking for you is no more than an eight-year-old child. Do you know some adults who act like two-year-olds? Probably lots, and that's because they are still acting out some major event that occurred when they were at that age. When working with people as a coach, I find it useful to frequently remind myself that the person I am interacting with is often a five-year-old trapped in a big body. You might want to consider doing the same.

What can you do with this information right now? Nothing . . . yet. It's simply something to think about, but it's also something that will be extremely relevant to the rest of this discussion. So for now, I just want you to entertain the thought that you live in a conversation, that within that conversation is your paradigm, and that what makes you *you* is that conversation.

And above all else, remember *it's just a conversation.*

*Chapter 4*

# The Nature of Our Reality

HAVING ESTABLISHED that we live in a conversation, let's look at the nature of our reality and how we use language in the existing paradigm.

We wake up in the morning, look out into our world, and observe what we observe. We take in whatever we see, whatever is occurring at the time, and, as the observer, we have an explanation for what we see. Realize that I use the word "world" to encompass everything we see: our company, our spouse, our children, our employees, the competition, the economy, and on and on.

While it is not the case with all people all of the time, most of us believe that our explanation is "the truth" – that "it" and "them" are the way we see "it" and "them." Think about that for a moment. Don't you think that your children, your parents, your spouse, your employees, your job, your business, the economy, the competition, etc. are the way you see them because that's how they actually are? "That's just the way (fill in the blank) is," we say.

You may not have ever thought about this before, and that's okay. Remember, the purpose of our time together is to get you to look at things that are right in front of you, that you may take for granted and may have never thought about, and see them in a new way. That's why I'm asking you to think about this now.

You are an intelligent person. You have eyes. You can see and process information. That's why you think what you see is real. To you, it's the truth. If you think about it, you will see that is exactly what happens.

So you think there is a reality and you see it. Then you open your mouth to speak about what you see, and you describe or "talk about" it. If you doubt you do this, spend a day listening to other people speak. If you listen to others without judging them, you will discover that in most instances, people use language to "talk about" or describe the world they think they see. And, they think they are speaking the truth!

For example, I have had hundreds of discussions with company executives in which I ask them to tell me about their company, their employees, the economy, the competition, and so on. In every case, they answer my questions as if they are relating "facts." Rarely do they realize they are doing this.

Just the other day I was talking to an old friend. I was sharing how much I have come to learn to enjoy people, how fun I find them to be, how gracious I think people mostly are, and how much I enjoy meeting new people (more about this later). He quickly replied, "Yes, but that's just on the surface. If you go below, you will find that all people are up to no good, they are devious, self seeking, and mostly dishonest. You really ought to watch yourself with people."

"Really?" I replied. "What has you say that?"

"That's just the truth about people. If you paid attention, you'd see that's the way they are."

I could see there was no point in arguing with him. He "knew" how people "are." I don't know what happened that caused him to reach that conclusion, but that's the conclusion he reached. And there was no other possibility. It wasn't *his* truth; it was *the* truth.

As the conversation that day continued, I discovered many more of his "truths." *All* politicians are crooked, the plan to rebuild the world trade center was ridiculous, exercise isn't fun, his children don't care about him, it takes "forever" to get medical devices approved by the government, and on and on and on. He stated everything not as an observation or an opinion, but as a fact.

But think about it. If there were a reality or "truth", and we all had the ability to accurately see and describe what was really there, then wouldn't everyone see and describe the same thing? Your immediate answer is probably "no," because you know that everyone doesn't see the same thing. But reread the question I asked. The answer, as I posed the question, is "of course." If there was a reality or "truth," and we all could see it, then we should, by definition, all see the same thing.

But the reality is that we all *don't* see the same thing. Everyone sees something different. Everyone has his or her own perception. And aren't there times when you are absolutely sure something or somebody is a particular way, and you need to get others to see "it" or "them" that way, but they just don't? They are convinced that it's another way, because they are different observers.

If you think about this logically, then what I'm saying will be evident. We all see what we see, for reasons we will explore in a moment, and that's just the way it is. Everyone lives in a different reality. Everyone sees the world through a unique set of eyes. Therefore, does it make sense to use language to describe or "talk about" what's there? After all, who knows what's really there? There's only what you observe. So if you use language *only* to describe what *you* observe, with no attachment to whether it's the truth, then there's no harm done. However, that rarely occurs.

**Truth or Perception?**

So what's really going on? What is the nature of our reality? And, what is the true function of language? Consider this possibility: We wake up in the morning, look out into our world, and see what we see, just as we've discussed before. There is still something going on, some phenomenon. And you are still the observer.

But what makes you the observer you are? What do you wake up into? The answer is that "conversation" – the one that has been developing since day one. And here's what I'm suggesting actually happens, and you can look at it in one of two ways. Specifically, you either:

- Project your conversation onto the world you see, and see your individualized version of whatever is there; or
- You interpret what you observe through a filtering mechanism that your conversation controls.

Are you with me? Here's an example: You have an employee, and your conversation is that he's lazy. Is that "the truth?" Who knows? You certainly have evidence that he's lazy, but that "evidence" could justify any one of a number of other conclusions. Perhaps his wife isn't well and he's preoccupied at the moment with her health. Maybe his kids are having problems in school. Perhaps he's going through a divorce. Who knows? All you know is that he acts in a certain way, and you've interpreted his behavior as being lazy.

So you walk into work in the morning, and there he is – that lazy guy. Then you have conversations with others about what to do with this lazy employee. And even if he works hard one day, you think he's up to something, because, after all, he's lazy. In your world, he just is that way.

Here's another example: In the early '80s, interest rates rose to 18+%. Lots of people got out of the real estate business because they assumed that with interest rates that high, nobody would be buying houses, and it would be impossible to make a sale. Their interpretation of the events of the day told them to quit the business because there was nothing they could do to change the situation.

Yet, I know someone who came to this country from India right at this time and decided to get into the real estate business. Over the next few years, while many were fleeing from the business, he became rich. Why? He didn't realize that interest rates weren't always at that level and he was committed to being successful. All he saw was opportunities, not impossibilities.

What I'm now asking you to consider is that there is no world "out there" that *is* a particular way. There is no "reality." Yes, there is some physical, objective reality, such as the person who works for you, interest rates, the economy, etc., but we don't relate to those *things*. We only relate to our *interpretation* and our *explanation* of what we see.

So is what we are seeing the "the truth" or our interpretation? I say it's *always* our interpretation – that is, *you* are the source of what you see. You interpret everything based on how you learned to interpret things when you were young, filtering everything through your conversation, and that's why everyone has different opinions and perceptions. It's not that there's something different out there for everyone to see; rather, everyone is a different observer and interprets things differently.

## The True Function of Language

This brings us back to language and its function. If language's purpose is not to talk about or describe what is there, then what *is* its function?

When I ask this question in a workshop or a speech, the answers I receive are usually quite funny, at least to me. The most common answer is "to convince others that what we see is really the truth." We certainly do that. Another is "to share our reality." Sometimes we do that as well. Some people say, "to express our opinion (which we rarely 'own' as just our opinion; we usually speak our opinion as 'the truth')." Another common answer is "to ask questions so we can find out what other people see." All of these responses are valid uses of language.

What I want you to consider, though, is that the fundamental purpose of language is to create and invent with. Language is primarily a tool of creation. You are the source of what you see – it's all your interpretation – and every time you open your mouth, you are *not describing* what's there; rather, you are speaking into existence what's there, *for you*. No, it's not *the truth*; it's only *your truth!* We don't describe the world we see – we see the world we describe!

## You Create Your Reality Every Time You Open Your Mouth

Imagine you and I are walking in the woods. We come around the bend in the trail, and standing right in front of us is a big black bear.

What's your conversation? Most people answer: "Oh my God! What am I going to do? This is scary! Should I run, play dead, yell for help?" And because that is their conversation, their reaction is one of fear.

I remember the first time this actually happened to me. It was 1980, and I was backpacking with a friend in Yosemite National Park. We had hiked up the trail from Tenaya Lake and were on our way to Sunrise High Sierra Camp, where we were going to spend the night.

For some reason, my friend and I got separated, and I was walking alone along the trail. I came around a bend in the trail, and there in front of me, no more than ten yards away, was a big black bear. I stopped, and then the excitement of the moment hit me. To be that close to a bear in the wilderness was thrilling. I was not the slightest bit scared. I had thought about the possibility of this moment in advance and *my* conversation was that, for the most part, bears are friendly. They want your food, not you, and as long as you don't do anything stupid, you have nothing to worry about.

What's "the truth?" Should you be afraid or excited? Are bears scary and dangerous, or are they playful, cute and safe? I don't know. And I don't care. I only know what's true for me. And what's true for me is whatever I say!

The same goes for you. What's true for you, *in every area of your life and your business,* is whatever *you* say. It's important to understand this, because our actions are always in response to the world we see. Unfortunately, we don't realize that *we* literally make up the world we see, and that we do it with language.

(By the way, the bear didn't attack me or do anything threatening. It looked at me for a moment and then went on with its business, walking back into the woods, leaving me wanting more.)

### Life is Like a Tennis Game

An analogy might be helpful at this point. Think of a tennis match. In any game of tennis, there is a very different game going on in the stands than the game being played on the court. In the stands, the people watching the game have a conversation that goes something like this: "Boy, does he have a great forehand! His backhand is a bit weak, but his serve is really good. And look how quickly he gets to the net. Wow! What an overhead, etc."

In the stands, there are forehands and backhands and serves and overheads. But that's not what's happening on the court. On the court, the player is following the ball and trying his or her best to hit it over the net. If he is standing on one side of the court and the opponent hits the ball to the other side, he runs over there and hits the ball. If the opponent hits a drop shot, he runs forward and hits the ball. And so it goes.

On the court, there are no forehands, no backhands, and no overheads. Everyone who has ever played tennis knows that. There's just a player following the ball and trying to hit it. The player's actions are always in reaction to how the ball shows up *to the player* as it comes across the net.

Many years ago Stefan Edberg played Boris Becker in the finals at Wimbledon. Stefan Edberg won the match. As I watched him play, I remember thinking that he must be in "the zone" I've heard athletes talk about, because he played so well. As he left the court after his win, Bud Collins approached him for an interview. He asked Stefan what it was like for him during the match and why he thought he played so well.

Stefan's response is something I'll never forget. He said, "As the match wore on, the ball got bigger and bigger, and it came across the net slower and slower. I got to the point where I knew I would make every shot."

What was Stefan doing? He was responding to how the ball showed up, and that's what happens on the court in any tennis match.

As a former tennis player, I think about what it would be like for me standing on a tennis court with Andy Roddick serving the ball at 140+ miles per hour. The ball would likely look like a pea shot out of a cannon. But for today's great tennis players, they see something quite different, something akin to what Stefan Edberg saw in his match with Boris Becker, and so they often have little difficulty returning Andy's serve.

The same thing happens in the game of life. Our actions are always in response to how the world in front of us shows up for us (and, again, I use the word "world" to refer to whatever is in front of us at the moment). So our actions in business are in response to how our employees, our competitors, the economy, and on and on show up for us. I hope this is evident.

What may not be evident is that we mostly think it's "them" or "it" (our competitors or our employees, for example) that is having them or it show up for us the way they do. So we think the economy "is" a particular way, and that's why it occurs for us the way it does. The same happens with our business, the competition, our employees, etc. And, as stated previously, we use language to describe or talk about the way our business, the competition, the economy, etc, is.

This mentality is like continuing to live as if the earth were flat, when we now know that it is round. What's worse is that this thinking turns you into a victim. You believe that events are outside the realm of your control and that your only choice is to react or respond to circumstances that someone or something else created.

To the contrary, I'm suggesting that *you* are determining the way your world shows up for you. As I said previously, you are either projecting the conversation that you have about whatever or whomever is in front of you onto what's there or filtering whatever you see through that conversation. So, when you open your mouth and talk about the economy, your business, the competition, whatever, you are actually speaking that reality into existence. Then you act on it as if it were the truth. But it's only the truth for you, and only because you thought and said it!

This is the first and most important attribute of the new paradigm leader we are creating. Being a powerful, effective, and "conscious" leader means:

* You realize that what you see is your perception;
* You understand that you are creating your perception all the time; you do it whenever you open your mouth to speak;
* You are responsible for what you say; and
* You accept the consequences of what you think and speak.

Other attributes are the flip side of the above points:

* You realize that what other people say is merely their perception;
* You understand that what comes out of their mouth is only their truth, whether they realize it or not;
* You hold them responsible for what they say; and
* You allow them to accept the consequences for what they think and speak.

## Creating Your Reality

Your tongue is like a paintbrush. Every time you open your mouth, you paint a picture of a world, and then you AND EVERYONE AROUND YOU live into that world as if it were the truth. But it's not *the* truth; it's only *your* truth. Now the question is, are you doing this responsibly and thinking deeply about what you say and how you say it, or are you doing it unconsciously and irresponsibly?

Consider that about six billion people live on the planet and that there are six billion different realities. Everyone's "reality" is, in a very true sense, a figment of his or her imagination. And so few people actually see this. Consider my friend who exemplifies this point. He actually thought that what he was saying about people is "the truth." If I even suggested that maybe it wasn't *the* truth, just *his* truth, he'd be insulted and get defensive. And he's not unique. I'm asking you to look at the extent to which you do the same thing!

When you think your explanation of what's going on in front of you is the "truth," that's the end of the discussion. If you're committed to your point of view, you're stuck. But if you realize that it's all your interpretation, that it's all up for discussion, then you have power.

Because how we explain and interpret the world we live in usually leads to very different courses of action. Suppose your daughter comes home from school with a bad report card. Lots of explanations are available: she's not smart, she's lazy, her friends are a bad influence, she has a lousy teacher, etc. The explanation you give yourself determines the course of action you take.

If you think she's not very smart, you get her a tutor. If you think she's lazy, you do what you can to motivate her. If you think her friends are a bad influence, you try to convince her to find new friends. If you think she has a lousy teacher, you likely go talk to the teacher or the principal. This is precisely why it's crucial to understand that these are all interpretations, and being a conscious observer is key.

*Chapter 5*

# The Nature of Satisfaction and Happiness

THERE ARE so many examples of why it is essential to understand that you use language for creation rather than description that the list is almost endless. For instance, let's explore the nature of satisfaction.

How do you normally determine whether you're satisfied? For most people, satisfaction is determined by how they view the circumstances they experience. In other words, we look at our circumstances, judge whether the circumstances are the way we would like them to be, and if they are we're satisfied and if they're not we're dissatisfied.

When you live this way, your circumstances determine your satisfaction. You're like a weather vane in a storm, with your level of satisfaction being at the whim of your life's circumstances.

Consider that in any given situation, your inner conversation or thoughts can be anything. You can be desperately poor and profoundly satisfied, or fabulously wealthy and completely miserable. It's all a matter of what you think and how you *choose to interpret* your circumstances.

So what if you decide to start from a state of satisfaction? What if you decide that your life is whatever it is, that you're satisfied, and then go forth from there? Think how wonderful it would be to stop trying so hard to get to satisfaction. Imagine how much more powerful it would be to start from a state of satisfaction and then take your satisfaction with you wherever you go.

## A Fundamental Reality of Life

Now, here's the real rub. You can't get to any place other than where you start from, and that is another fundamental principle the new paradigm leader we are creating realizes. In other words, if you "say" you're dissatisfied, for whatever reason, likely because you don't like your circumstances, and then set out to get to satisfaction, what do you take with you every step of the way? Dissatisfaction! With such baggage, you'll never know when you arrive at your destination. Your experience will be like the proverbial hamster on a tread wheel. No matter how good the circumstances get, you're always seeking more and better, because you're standing in a place of dissatisfaction.

Yes, sometimes things just seem to click and you say "this is it," but how long does that last? Usually, not very long. You soon find yourself back in a place of dissatisfaction. It would be a lot easier and a lot more fun to decide, right here and right now, that you're satisfied and then take that mindset with you on your journey into the future.

How can you develop such a mindset? Here's a start: Consider that if you had the money to buy this book, you're one of the luckier people alive. Over 30,000 people die every day from starvation. Millions of people around the world live in poverty. Half the people on the planet have never used a telephone, and a lot more don't have computers or cell phones or fax machines – all those wonderful modern conveniences we take for granted. So when you step back and look at the condition of our planet, it only makes sense to be profoundly grateful for how wonderful our lives truly are.

By the way, this is not about "positive thinking." Every day people die, planes crash, accidents happen, crimes occur, and people do bad things to each other. I'm not ignoring the realities of life. Fortunately, there's plenty of room in the context of satisfaction for the entire range of human emotions. Will you be satisfied all the time? Of course not. But when you're committed to being satisfied, you take your licks and rebound a lot faster; you get over the sadness or the hurt or the anger, and you get back to doing your work. Rather than being about positive thinking, this discussion is about taking responsibility for your life and not being a victim.

I remember clearly one day several months ago. I started the day with the news that a prospective client decided to proceed with the project we had discussed. I was elated. A short time later, a speech I thought I would get was given to someone else. I had really thought I would be the one and had worked hard to get the engagement. I was frustrated and disappointed. Sometime later in the day, somebody I considered to be a friend made a remark I thought was insulting and I was angry. And to top it all off, I received an e-mail that my cousin, who had been battling a life threatening disease for quite awhile, had died.

As I hope you can imagine, there are many ways to interpret such a day. In the past, I would probably have said

something like, "Oh well, you win some and you lose some."
For what I liked, I would have said it was "good," and for what
I didn't like, I would have said it was "bad." I remember this
day so clearly because that's not how I looked at the day.
Given my commitment to be satisfied, I remember saying to
myself, "What an amazing day. What a gift it is to be alive. In
one day I experienced the entire range of human emotions.
One minute I was thrilled, the next disappointed, the next angry, the next sad, and then back to being thrilled. Wow! How
extraordinary. How blessed I am to have such freedom."
Strange? No. Different? Surely.

When you put these ideas into practice, you set a wonderful example, which is one of the keys to empowering leadership. Remember, your tongue is like a paintbrush. Every time
you open your mouth, you paint a picture of a world and then
you AND EVERYONE AROUND YOU live into that world as
if it were the truth. So if you're satisfied and grateful, then
words of satisfaction and gratitude come out of your mouth,
which is highly motivating to the people around you. Satisfaction and gratitude are contagious.

But, unfortunately, dissatisfaction and complaining are
also contagious. So if words of dissatisfaction and complaints
come out of your mouth, then you will be de-motivating the
people around you. Which mindset do you choose?

## Happiness

Another example that demonstrates what I'm asking you to
consider, that language is a vehicle of creation, is the nature of
happiness. How do you normally determine whether you are
happy? In our Western culture, many people think they will

be happy when they achieve the "American Dream." You know – the house with the white picket fence, the Mercedes, the weekend cottage at the lake, etc. And Madison Avenue knows how desperately we want this dream life. That's why all advertising is an attempt to convince us we will be a lot happier if we use the product or service they are promoting.

I'm suggesting that happiness, like satisfaction, has little or nothing to do with our circumstances. The fact is that either you're willing to be happy or you're not. It's a choice you make. Just like satisfaction, happiness lives in your conversation. In her book *Real Moments* (Dell Publishing, 1994), Barbara DeAngeles, Ph.D. says, "Happiness is a choice you make in each moment about how you experience that moment, not a state you one day achieve." So you either choose to be happy or you don't. And your choice is reflected in what you say.

One day while I was giving a speech, some words slipped out of my mouth that I had never spoken before. I'm not sure where the thought came from, but I have repeated it numerous times ever since. What I said is that at any given moment, 99.9999.% of the things in our lives are working absolutely perfectly. The earth keeps rotating around its axis every day, staying exactly the right distance from the sun so we don't get too hot or too cold. Fresh air is all around for us to breathe. Our heart and other organs do their thing. All these events happen without any input from us.

From that perspective, it must follow that only .0001% of the things in our lives are not working absolutely perfectly. With that in mind, where do we so often focus our attention? Instead of waking up in the morning and saying, "Another day in paradise," noticing the 99.9999+% of the things that are working perfectly, without any input from us, and being grateful for the sheer privilege it is to be alive, we focus on and complain about the .0001% of the things that are not the way we want them to be. Unbelievable? Yes. But it is true. Sometimes I think we are truly insane.

Recently, at a speech I gave at a convention in Las Vegas, I asked the attendees, "How many of you wake up in the morning in a conversation of 'another day in paradise'?" No hands went up. When you stop to think about it, isn't that sad?

At any moment, regardless of the circumstances, you can choose to be happy and satisfied, to appreciate and feel grateful for what you already have, and to stop waiting for life to turn out better. Because you know what? Your life has already turned out. And this is what it looks like when it turns out. This. Right now. It all lives in your thinking and your conversation.

So this is it. Choose. Are you satisfied or not? Are you happy or not? As a leader, your choice impacts not only you, but also everyone in your organization and the organization itself. It's an important choice, so choose wisely. And remember, it all lives in your conversation.

*Chapter 6*

# Our Relationship to People

IN ALL of our relationships, how we use language, once again, creates our reality. Here's how it works. In the ordinary course of events, how we relate to people is we judge and assess them. We meet someone, and within the first few seconds we make some judgment and/or assessment about him or her. No wonder you don't get a second chance to make a good first impression.

In workshops and speeches, I ask people to say some of the not-so-nice words they have heard come out of their mouths during this process of judging and assessing people. The list that evolves includes jerk, idiot, ugly, cheap, lazy, arrogant, self-centered, selfish, stupid, impatient, dishonest, incompetent, inconsiderate, and on and on. Some of the things people say are not fit to print. In any event, it's not a pretty list. Have you heard yourself use some or all of these words?

Then I ask, "What's possible in how we relate to people?" Given that language creates our reality, couldn't we invent who people are? What a novel concept. The question then becomes, "What are some of the empowering words we *could* say about people?" The list that evolves includes wonderful, smart, clever, honest, talented, creative, team player, contributor, caring, patient, generous, brilliant, loving, gorgeous, fabulous, and on and on.

At this moment, I ask the $64,000 question: "What's the 'truth' about people?" Some of the answers are "a little of both," "someplace in the middle," "depends," "sometimes one and sometimes the other," and answers like that. What's your answer?

I say that there is no "truth" about people. Better yet, I don't know what the truth is about people. I'm not that smart. Do you know what "the truth" is? I only know what's true for me. And I suggest that what's true for you is what's true only for you. And your truth is what *you* decide!

## Golden Wisdom

My first insight into what I am suggesting came in the late 1980s. I had a coaching company and received a contract to work with and coach thirty real estate agents in an office that was not doing well. I did the project as a joint venture with Amba Gale, the owner of another coaching company. Together, we produced dramatic results. In five months, the average agent increased productivity by approximately 300%, and this office went from being the least profitable in the region to the most profitable in the state.

The regional VP was so thrilled with the results that he hired us to work with the other offices in the region. Amba didn't personally want to continue with the project, so she sent one of her employees, Rita Reneaux, to work with me on future projects.

On the first day of the next project, Rita and I stood at the front of the room as the agents walked in for their first coaching session. As always, and without realizing I was doing so, I made my usual judgments and assessments of each person. Yet I couldn't help but notice how excited Rita was becoming as each person entered. I couldn't imagine what was going on with her. But we did what we were there to do that day, and I left her conduct for a future discussion.

At the end of the day, I turned to Rita and asked, "What was going on with you this morning when the people were coming into the room?"

She looked at me quizzically and replied, "What are you talking about?"

So I said, "Well, when the people were coming in, I saw you getting more and more excited by the minute, and I couldn't understand why. They looked like a pretty ragged group to me; some even seemed unfriendly. I thought we were going to have quite a time working with this group, but you didn't seem to have the same thoughts at all."

Finally understanding what my question was, she smiled and said, "I saw one more wonderful person after another coming in the room, and that's why I was so excited."

I looked at her in amazement and jokingly asked, "Are you on drugs or something? One more wonderful person after another? Are you kidding?"

Understanding my confusion, she said, "Scott, if you went looking for gold, would you find it lying on the ground, or would you have to dig in the dirt to find it?"

"Well," I replied, "you would likely have to dig in the dirt for it."

Then she said something that would ultimately change my life: "People are the same way. Inside of *every* human being is a bar of solid gold. But it's often covered up with all kinds of 'dirt' they picked up when they were two and three and four and fourteen years old. Now the question is, 'What will you go looking for?' Whatever it is, I promise you will always find it. If you stop looking when you see the dirt, so be it. But if you look deeply, you'll almost always find the gold!"

I recently heard a different version of the same story. One hundred years ago, Andrew Carnegie, the first great American industrialist, had forty-three millionaires on his payroll. A reporter interviewing him asked how he was able to employ that many millionaires. His answer was that none of them were millionaires when they first came to work for him. The reporter then asked how he was able to develop these people so that they became so valuable that he could afford to pay them enough to become millionaires. Carnegie's answer was that you develop people the same way you mine for gold. When you go into a mine, you expect to remove a ton of dirt for every ounce of gold. But the secret is that you go looking for the gold, not the dirt!

So I'm inviting you to consider that there is no "truth" about people. There's only what's true for you. If you give yourself permission to judge and assess people, you'll only see your own judgments and assessments. But if you decide in advance that all people are brilliant, gorgeous, talented, and fabulous, and go looking for that, then that's what you will see far more often.

## Some Important Principles

That day, Rita got me thinking deeply into this subject, and I have come, many years later, to understand four powerful principles. What I mean by a "principle" is something that works not just some of the time, but *all* of the time. It's like gravity – if you drop something, it goes down, every single time. That's why it's a principle.

### Principle #1: *You will always find what you go looking for*

If you think the world is full of jerks, you'll find lots of them. If you think people are wonderful, you'll find a lot of wonderful people.

Now you might say, "Yes, but you don't know _____ (insert any name here). He really *is* a jerk!"

I say he isn't. I say he is a brilliant, gorgeous, talented, fabulous person who, for some reason, because of some belief, *at times,* may act like a jerk. But do you see him all of the time? How do you know how he acts in different situations and with different people? And, because you've labeled him a jerk, you won't see all of the times that he doesn't act that way.

Someone reading what I just wrote recently asked me an interesting question. He asked, "So if you don't find what you go looking for does that mean you're looking in the wrong place?"

"No," I said, "you're missing the point. This is not about looking for a 'thing' and wondering why you can't find it. This is a principle in life. If you think people are great, you'll see lots of great people. If you think your business has lots of opportunities for success, you'll find opportunities. If you think that you have lots of problems, you'll find problems all over the place."

Many years ago I worked with the partners of a large law firm headquartered in San Francisco. My project with them lasted for six months, so I got to know all of the partners well. When the job was complete, the firm's chairman took me aside and said, "You have to help me do something with John (not his real name). He's the manager of the Los Angeles office and he has everyone upset. He's a great lawyer, but he's angry all of the time, and I'm about to have a revolt down there."

I looked into the situation, talked to many of the associates in the Los Angeles office, and found that what I was told was the truth. They all thought John was some version of "jerk." I don't remember their exact words, but none of them liked him. They thought he was awful to deal with, that he yelled all the time, and that he needed to go. They were at the point where if he didn't leave, they would.

I was stunned. I had worked with John for six months and found him to be a gracious, compassionate, and generally friendly guy. Was I crazy? Why didn't I see his "jerk" factor? I decided to meet with John. It was a meeting I'll never forget. Here's how it went.

I started by saying, "John, I hear that you get angry a lot and yell at people. Is that the truth?"

He hesitated for a moment and then somewhat sheepishly replied, "Yes, I guess it is."

Sensing his willingness to be open, I asked, "Well, why do you do that?"

His answer was interesting. He said, "Well, I have this group of really smart, talented lawyers that work in this office. I don't see any of them living up to their potential. Sometimes it seems like they do just enough to get by, and it really irritates me."

I could have gone down the tunnel of saying, "Boy, what a jerk!" But given my "conversation" that all people are wonderful and *almost always* have a good motive for what they do, and looking for that, I heard something that I thought would get me to the bottom of his behavior. My reply was, "So, you have these people around you who you don't see living up to the potential you see in them, and you think that getting angry and yelling will motivate them to get into action and do the job you think they are capable of!"

He looked right back at me and said, "You know, I never thought about it that way. But now that I hear what you just said, I'd say you were exactly right." (By the way, these are the things you hear when you look for the gold that you never hear when you judge and assess people and call them a jerk.)

I then said, "Interesting strategy. Does it work?"

"Heck no," he said. "And what's worse is that they hate me."

So I said, "Why do you continue doing it?"

He replied, "I don't know what else to do!"

Do you get it? He had a legitimate objective, to motivate his staff to fulfill their potential, but he had come up with an unworkable strategy to meet his objective. The more he tried to implement the strategy, the less it worked. The result was that the people around him saw him as a "jerk," not as a good guy with a bad strategy. Had they been trained to look for the gold, as I'm asking you to do, they could have had the same conversation with him that I did, and I wouldn't have had to get involved.

Such a scenario is typical with people. They develop ineffective strategies, probably at age four or five, to accomplish legitimate objectives, and continue to play out those strategies despite the negative outcomes. They then get more and more frustrated along the way, even though they know it's not working, *because they just don't know what else to do!* And instead of us being compassionate and understanding, given the pain they must be in, we label them jerk, idiot, arrogant, etc, and the game is over. (I'll talk more in Chapter 12 about what the payoff is for us when we do that and what it costs us.)

Getting back to John, I next said to him, "If I could show you a strategy that was designed to accomplish your legitimate objective, eliminate your need to get angry, and actually have people like you, would you be interested?"

"Of course," he said.

So I took out a piece of paper and drew two parallel lines representing the two sides of a river. Between them I drew a few squiggly lines representing the water. I then said, "Let's make believe the lawyers in your office are standing on one side of this river and you want to get them to the other side. And let's say that the water is ice cold and running too fast for them to swim. Can you see that no amount of yelling will get them to jump in and swim to the other side?"

"Sure," he said.

I continued, "Suppose we put a bunch of big rocks in the river, close together, so it wouldn't be too difficult to get from one to the other, and put them all the way across. Now, what if you told them to step on only the first rock? What if you assured them that you had all the confidence in the world in their ability to do that, to not worry about the rest of the rocks, and to focus only on the first rock and give it a try. Do you think they would do that?"

Again, he said, "Sure."

"Okay. What if, when they got on the first rock, you congratulate them, tell them how much you knew they could do it, how proud you are of them, and how much you appreciate their courage and willingness to take that first step? Do you think they would feel good about themselves, or perhaps have a new found confidence in themselves?"

"I would imagine so," he replied.

"Great. I think so too. Now, what if you told them to step on the second rock, again repeating what you said before? Do you think it might actually take less coaxing the second time?"

"Yes, I would think so," he answered.

"And what if you kept repeating this process, over and over again? Do you see the possibility of getting them to the other side? And throughout it all, you never got angry and never yelled. With every step of the way, their confidence got greater and greater, and they actually fulfilled the potential you saw in them."

Now John was excited. This entire conversation lasted less than two hours, and he was ready to get into action. We shook hands, and I asked him to call me in two weeks to let me know how it was going.

Two weeks later I got an excited phone call from John. He said, "Scott, this has been a fabulous two weeks. I've had some really great conversations with my lawyers. I haven't gotten angry once, haven't yelled, and they are even starting to ask me to go to lunch with them." (Something they used to avoid like the plague.)

"Congratulations!" I said. "Keep up the good work. And let me know if you have any problems."

I never heard from him again. I did, however, receive a call about a month after my meeting with John from the chairman in San Francisco. His opening line was, "What did you do to John?"

I had to laugh at the way he asked the question. "What do you mean?" I asked.

"I called down there the other day to find out if anyone had left and spoke to several of the associates. They all said that the problem with John had miraculously been resolved, that he was being wonderful and supportive, and that they were all happy campers."

You can imagine how I felt. Not wanting to tell stories out of school, I simply said, "I knew John was a good guy. You asked me to find out what the problem was, so I did. We put in the correction, and that should be the end of that. If you have any other problems, please let me know."

He thanked me profusely, and that *was* the end of that.

So I again invite you to consider that there is no "truth" about people. There's only what's true for you. People have the ability to be everything from wonderful to awful. You could say they are pure potential. And if you give yourself permission to judge and assess them, you'll see all of your judgments and assessments. But if you decide in advance that all people are brilliant, gorgeous, talented, and fabulous, and go looking for the gold, then that's what you will see far more often.

### Principle #2: People "show up" around you based on who you believe them to be

This principle may be tougher to appreciate right away, but consider this: Do you notice that around some people you act one way, and around others you act completely different? And haven't you had discussions with someone about a third person you both knew and found that the other party's opinion and impression of the third person was so different from yours that you could hardly believe you were talking about the same person?

This occurs because of Principle #2. We do not live in a vacuum. The beliefs people have about us (which live in their conversations about us) influence who we are around them in dramatic and almost amazing ways. For me, when I'm around clients who think I'm brilliant, I find myself saying the most brilliant things. Yet around people who, for one reason or another, have judgments about me, I find myself being totally consistent with their judgments, far from being brilliant.

For example, being patient is not one of my strengths. In fact, I have an extraordinary capability to be impatient. I'm aware of this and work very hard at being patient. And, because of my awareness, I'm far more patient than I've ever been.

When I'm around people who know me well, who have no judgments about my behavior, and who don't make me wrong about how I act, I actually find myself being much more peaceful and almost amazingly patient. But once in awhile, when I meet someone new who sees some behavior that they interpret as impatient, I start becoming impatient. As their judgment of me increases, as I become for them this impatient person, I become increasingly impatient. It's like a snowball rolling down hill. And what's worse, I see my own behavior and find myself incapable of stopping it.

Psychologists verify this principle. For example, if there is a "problem child" in a family, the old school was to send the child to the psychologist. But they found that as long as the family related to the child as a "problem," then that's how the child continued to be. Today, many psychologists will work instead with the entire family. Once they all agree to stop relating to the child as a "problem" and to start relating to him or her as some version of brilliant, gorgeous, talented, and fabulous, more often than not, the problem goes away.

A coach once told me a story about a company she worked with that did work for the United States government, which again clearly demonstrates this principle. The company's main contact in the government was an army general. For the people in the company who worked with him, the relationship was a nightmare. They thought he was a "wall" they had to hurdle on every procurement. They had nothing nice to say about him. To them, he was a roadblock and a "problem." They hired the coach to help them deal with him.

The coaching was not what they expected. She got all the people together who had anything to do with the general and said to them, "I invite you to try an experiment for one month. If it doesn't work, we'll try something different, but here's what I want you to do. For the next month, I request that you change your conversation about the general. Let's make believe that this general is not a problem, that he doesn't enjoy making your life miserable. Let's further make believe that he is a wonderful man, that he deeply loves his country, and that all he thinks about is doing the very best job he knows how to make sure the interests of the government he so much loves are served. Let's also make believe that he wants to work with you just as much as you want to work with him, that he likes you and your company, that he believes what you do is good for the country, and that his only reservation in any deal is that the country's interests are served."

Her words were a hard sell, because none of what she said was their experience of the general. But she convinced them to give it a try for a month, with one condition on her part: They really had to take it on. No faking it. They had to take on her description totally and without reservation and play it out fully for one month. They agreed. They even agreed to have fun doing it.

She left and didn't come back or have any contact with them for the month. When she returned to the company and brought the team together, they all said, almost in unison, "What did you do to the general?"

"What do you mean?" she replied.

"You got to the general, didn't you?" they suspiciously asked.

"Absolutely not!" she said. "What makes you think that?"

"He's been fabulous. He's working with us and cooperating. We got through several bids without incident. It's been like night and day."

Principle #2 at work: People "show up" around you based on who you believe them to be/your conversation about them.

What an advantage you could have and what a powerful and effective leader you could be if you fully embraced this distinction and took responsibility for these two principles.

### Principle #3: Who people are and how they behave are separate and distinct

We create a lot of mischief when we don't honor this principle. What I'm suggesting, as I've said before, is that inside everyone is a bar of solid gold, but it's often covered up with behaviors based on decisions made a long time ago, ineffective strategies designed to accomplish legitimate results.

But rather than speaking to the person's behavior only, while acknowledging that they are, in reality, a decent human being, we collapse the two and speak as if their behavior is who they are.

My experience is that parents do this quite frequently with their children, with quite damaging results. I remember vividly a situation that occurred on a recent business trip that demonstrates what I am speaking about. I was sitting outside a gate at the Dallas-Fort Worth airport waiting for a connection that was running late. The waiting area was filled with people, including a young couple and their daughter who I estimated to be about five years old.

Most of us were reading, relaxing, talking to each other, but not the little girl. She was just a beehive of activity. The father, thinking that she was probably annoying people, kept trying to get her to relax, with little success. I so much wanted to go over to him and say: "It's really all right. She's just being a five-year-old and doing what a five-year-old does. You can't expect her to sit and read USA Today!" But I didn't. In hindsight, I'm sorry for that.

Here's what happened next: In his final attempt to get her to stop what she was doing, he called her over and said, "I'm sorry but the plane will be here shortly and you will not be permitted to get on." Not understanding, she looked at her father and asked, "Why not?" His answer was, "They only allow good little girls on the plane."

She slumped down on the floor and began to cry. He had finally accomplished his objective, but at what price? Rather than speaking only about her behavior and honoring her as a human being, he labeled her "bad." And don't we do this all the time?

Had he understood principle #3, he might have said something like: "You are a fabulous, wonderful, playful, joyous little girl, and I love you deeply. I appreciate how much you love to play and have fun. And, there are times when your playfulness might be disrupting to others who have other things to do. This may be one of those times. There are many people in this small area waiting for this plane, some are reading, others are having conversations. I would appreciate it if you would, just for a few minutes, tone down your playfulness so that you don't disturb anyone. Would you be willing to do that?" Or, even better yet, he could have said nothing and just let her be five years old. She really wasn't bothering any of us.

The failure to notice this principle plays out every day at work. We label people lazy, inconsiderate, uncommitted, and on and on, rather than honoring the fundamental goodness in people and focusing our criticisms and concerns on their behavior. As leaders, we need to understand and operate consistent with this principle too.

*Principle #4: There's nobody "out there" other than a*
*reflection of you*

I have come to believe that every single person who enters our
lives primarily serves as an opportunity to discover who we
are. Another way of saying this is that every relationship, no
matter how brief or intimate, is designed to teach us something, and the person is our teacher.

It's like each person holds up a mirror so that we can see
who *we* are. Are we being gracious, loving, and accepting, or
are we being judgmental, critical, and fault-finding? Are we
seeing the gold or the dirt? When we see people who we like,
we are seeing in them those parts of ourselves that we like and
are at peace with. But when we see people who we don't like,
we are seeing in them our own shortcomings, those parts of
ourselves that we do not accept or are not at peace about.

Also, as we will discuss later on, when we are upset with
people, it never has anything to do with them. People upset us
only because they do not fulfill our expectations of them, they
are not the way we want them to be, they do not act the way we
want them to act, or they do not produce the results we want
them to produce.

This may not make sense to you or, at worse, you may
think this is ridiculous. But I assure you this is indeed a principle, and one that, if you are willing to consider and inquire
into, will serve you very well on your path to becoming the
leader we are here creating.

## A Personal Detour

Here's one last example to demonstrate these principles. Are you married? If not, are you living with someone? Or, do you have a significant other in your life? In any event, the statistics regarding personal relationships are disturbing. The probability is high that you are either unhappy in that relationship now or you will soon be unhappy, separated, or divorced! In fact, the divorce rate is still about 55% among first marriages and 70% among second marriages. And the majority of people who do stay together aren't necessarily thrilled with their relationship.

Why is this? Are people not compatible? Do they not know how to get along? I assert that in the vast majority of cases, people don't "invent" who their partner is. Rather, people get into personal relationships and do exactly what I have been explaining in this book. They have a picture of the way they think or would like their partner to be, and then they constantly judge and assess who that person is, to see if he or she is fitting that picture. On those rare occurrences when the partner does fit, they are happy. But unfortunately, far too often the other person doesn't fit. And so the cycle of the relationship's destruction begins as the disappointments mount one upon another.

And, when problems occur, the parties don't honor principle #3 and speak only of the other person's behavior. Rather, they all too frequently attack and make accusations about who the person is, which is as damaging to them as the comment the father made to the five-year-old was to her.

And, of course, by not appreciating principle #4, partners in a relationship don't treat the other as his or her teacher, nor do they realize that all the other person is doing is providing them an opportunity to become a more accepting, gracious, compassionate, and loving human being.

Would you like to stack the odds in your favor? Would you like to live happily ever after? It's really fairly simple. Stop judging your partner. Decide he or she is "the one." Invent the other person as brilliant, gorgeous, talented and fabulous. Look for the gold. Not only will that be what you will see far more often than not (principle #1 in action), but also he or she will become more brilliant, more gorgeous, and more fabulous every day (principle #2 in action).

## Time to Take Stock

What new ideas are opening up for you? What are you learning about you and/or your organization? Are you judging the people who work for you, or are you looking for the gold and inventing them as being brilliant, gorgeous, talented, and fabulous? What about them? Are they judging each other, making each other wrong, and being critical of each other, or are they inventing each other as being brilliant, gorgeous, talented, and fabulous? And what about your salespeople? Do they have judgments and assessments and opinions about your customers, or are they inventing them? I'd venture to guess that the former is the case in each scenario.

Can you see the limitations in that way of being? If you think your boss, your co-worker, your employee, or your customer is a jerk, then guess how he or she will show up? What's the likelihood you'll make the sale or get your point across when you're speaking to a jerk?

Consider the possibility that you have had far more control over the quality of your life and the quality of your relationships than you ever imagined. Consider the possibility that your satisfaction and your happiness have always been under your control, and you just never realized it. What an incredible opportunity you have to be satisfied, happy, and surrounded by brilliant, gorgeous, talented, and fabulous people.

How do you accomplish that? Remember that it's all just a conversation. You live in a conversation, you project that conversation onto the world, and then you live in it as if it were the truth. That's just the way it is. Now the question is, "Are you going to be at the effect of some conversation you created without much thought or consideration, probably a long time ago, or are you going to take responsibility for that conversation and create a world for yourself worth living in?"

## Speak It and Create It

Your tongue is like a paintbrush. Every time you open your mouth, you paint a picture for yourself and everybody around you to live in. As humans, we are usually unconscious about what comes out of our mouths. I'm asking you to stop that. Wake up. Listen to your thoughts and to the words that come out of your mouth. Decide in advance what you will say about everything and everybody. And then start saying that! It will change your world, your life, and the world and lives of all the people around you. Best of all, doing so will put you on the path to being a 21$^{st}$ Century leader.

In 1997 I got inspired to take what I'm saying seriously. I started a new document in my computer and titled it "My Highest Vision." Over the next year I created a picture, in words, of exactly who I would be if I were living in accordance with my highest and best vision for myself. I created the conversation I would live in as if it were the truth. It includes everything about who I would be, how I would act, what I would do, where I would live, what my relationships would be like, how I would feel, who people would be for me, my place in the world, the contribution I would be making, what my company would be like, and a lot more.

Then I started each day by carefully reading my new document, and I committed myself to living that day consistent with my vision. At the end of the day, I would review all of the day's events and see how I did. Each day I learned what I needed to work on. And I worked on it. It was the most useful exercise I have ever undertaken. And while I am not yet living my life in accordance with every aspect of my highest vision, I've come a long way. I invite you to do the same. If you would like a copy of my document to see what it looks like and to get you started, e mail me at scott@makingworkwork.com and I'll send it to you.

*Chapter 7*

# Cause and Effect

LET'S NOW take our discussion to a higher level. Consider the possibility that not only will your experience of life and your company be a function of your conversation, but that what you will *have* in your life and your company will also be a function of that conversation.

In the existing paradigm, you feel as if you have no control or impact on what happens "out there." Yes, you can *say* you're satisfied, and you can *say* you're happy, and you can *say* you relate to all people as if they are beautiful, gorgeous, talented, and fabulous. In the final analysis, though, you get what you get. At least that's what most people think.

Ever since Napolean Hill wrote *Think and Grow Rich,* and maybe even before then, people have been discussing the possibility that our thoughts attract the circumstances into our lives. In his book *You'll See It When You Believe It* (Harper Collins, 2001), the prolific author Dr. Wayne W. Dyer says that what you have in your life is a reflection of your beliefs. This notion has been popularized under the term "the power of positive thinking," the implication being that if you think "positive," you'll have a "positive" experience and produce "positive" results.

For many people, this was some "good idea" until Albert Einstein came along, whose theories gave birth to what is now known as quantum physics. As I understand it, Einstein said that the basic "stuff" of the universe is pure energy. But it's not any ordinary energy; rather, it's energy that has an intelligence to it. And, human thought activates it. This has given credibility to all the power of positive thinking theories.

So here's my understanding of the law of cause and effect and how this all relates. Simply stated, you are the "cause," and what manifests in your world is the "effect." More specifically, your thinking and beliefs determine how you become the "cause" in your company and your life.

Think of it as each of us being like a magnet. We attract things to ourselves that are consistent with our thinking and beliefs, and we repel things from ourselves that are inconsistent with our thinking and beliefs. Since it is highly unusual for someone to think, believe, speak, and act in ways that are fundamentally inconsistent, your conversation and your actions are a great access to your thinking and beliefs.

If you would like a more rigorous discussion of cause and effect than I am presenting here, as well as the work of the quantum physicists, I invite you to read *Quantum Physics, Illusion or Reality* by Alastair Rae, (Cambridge University Press, 1986), or *Quantum Legacy, The Discovery That Changed Our Universe,* by Barry Parker (Prometheus Books, 2002).

## You Get What You Think

Returning to our discussion about satisfaction, if you spend your days being satisfied and generating satisfaction in your conversation, then you will attract into your life circumstances and events that contribute to your satisfaction. Pretty great!

However, the converse is equally true. If you spend your days being dissatisfied and generating dissatisfaction in your conversation, then you will attract into your life circumstances and events that contribute to your dissatisfaction. The law of cause and effect is totally neutral. It doesn't care what you generate. It just responds.

The same applies for happiness. If you spend your days choosing to be happy and generating happiness in your conversation, then you will attract into your life circumstances and events that contribute to your happiness. Also pretty great!

The converse is true here too. If you spend your days choosing to be unhappy and generating unhappiness in your conversation, then you will attract into your life circumstances and events that contribute to your unhappiness.

This law applies in every area. If you think people are jerks, guess what you'll attract? Jerks! But if you think people are brilliant, gorgeous, talented, and fabulous, you'll attract brilliant, gorgeous, talented, and fabulous people. So consider that not only does your thinking and your speaking influence and/or create the way the world occurs for you, but it also *creates* how your world ultimately will be.

Here's a powerful way to relate to what I'm saying:

*Principle #5: You can't get anyplace other than where you start!*

So you can't get to satisfaction from dissatisfaction. If you're dissatisfied, you will attract into your life events and circumstances that contribute to your dissatisfaction. If you want to get to satisfaction, you have to start from satisfaction. It may sound crazy, but it's true. So you can't be unhappy and hope to one day be happy. You have to start from being happy.

Another way of saying it is that what you do doesn't matter. It's who you are "being" that counts. So be satisfied, be happy, be enthusiastic, be positive, be loving, be joyous (you get the point), and watch your world mirror those ways of being.

Can you now understand why I said what I did in Chapter 1, that I have noticed a common theme among all the successful companies: they consist of a group of enthusiastic, confident, positive people who work together on behalf of a future they have all committed themselves to? And can you now understand why I truly believe that this is the formula for success? If you have a group of enthusiastic, confident, positive people in your company, they will attract to the company opportunities and circumstances that contribute to that attitude. And, if everyone in your company is focused on a clearly identified future they have all committed themselves to, they will attract to the company all of the necessary circumstances that will contribute to that future becoming a reality!

Pretty extraordinary. Maybe all that strategic planning isn't the most important thing for you to be paying attention to after all. Same with all that emphasis on cost cutting, right sizing, down sizing, efficiency and all the other buzz words and popular fads. Just maybe, the key to your success is in creating an environment where people can be enthusiastic, confident, and positive and creating a future they can all be excited about and committed to.

Is all I've revealed thus far "the truth?" My best answer is that it's totally consistent with my experience working with people for over 18 years, and I invite you to find out for yourself.

### Fear

Here's another, profound consequence of not appreciating the law of cause and effect. If you look into our Western culture, what do you identify as the predominant human emotion? Sadness, happiness, joy, frustration, anger? When I ask people this question, under any circumstances, it rarely takes longer than five seconds for someone to answer *fear.*

And fear it is! Fear is the most prevalent of all human emotions. In fact, the book *A Course in Miracles,* and many other scholarly works, says that there are only two human emotions: love and fear. And anything that isn't love is fundamentally fear. Regardless of whether this is true, consider that at the very least, fear is a very common human emotion.

What's the opposite of fear? Well, we've already established that it's "love," but let's look at it from a more practical perspective. My favorite words that express the opposite of fear are *faith, trust,* and *optimism.* If we define fear as the expectation of an unfavorable or undesirable outcome, then faith, trust, and optimism all point to the expectation of a favorable or desirable outcome.

The fact that we live in a fear-based culture is so much a part of our paradigm that when we see or experience people who are overly happy, enthusiastic, and optimistic, we often call them a "Pollyanna" or naïve. We reason that since they think everything is wonderful, they certainly can't be in touch with "reality." Why do we call optimistic people a "Pollyanna"? Because fear is the biggest game in town – we just don't go around talking about it or admitting it. It's like water to the fish.

But it's important to bring fear up to the surface. If you "come from" a place of fear, meaning that you are fearful about something, then that is what you will project onto the world you live in and that is what you will see. Regardless of the real scariness or safety of any situation, if you believe there is something to fear, that's what your experience will be.

Haven't you encountered people who are afraid of something you consider to be totally safe? You may not be able to understand why they are afraid of it, but they are. It's their belief, and to them it's the truth.

For example, I'm a bicycling enthusiast, and I go on many bicycle trips. Often I have to climb long, steep hills. What keeps me going on those long uphills is the knowledge that sooner or later there will be a downhill . . . and I love those downhills. The steeper they are and the faster I can go, the better.

But I have ridden with many riders who, on those downhills, hold on to their brakes for dear life and descend very slowly. They believe going fast isn't safe. For me, it's safer to go fast than to hold onto your brakes, and I think they are missing all the fun. But going fast isn't fun for them; it's just plain scary.

The same is true with a bear in the woods. When some people encounter a bear, they pass out from fright. For me and others, it's an exciting experience.

So fear, like everything else, is just a conversation. It's an expectation, whether real or not, of an unfavorable outcome. To the fearful person, it's very real. And yet, it's just a conversation.

But here's the kicker. Given the law of cause and effect, if you are fearful, you will attract into your life and your company events and circumstances that support your fear. But remember that fear isn't bad; it's just like everything else in life. Its only use is to attract more of itself. So if you want to have a lot of things in your life that generate fear in you, be fearful!

Conversely, if you are optimistic, you will attract into your life and your company events and circumstances that support you in experiencing optimism. Optimism isn't *better* than fear; it just brings different consequences. The good news is that you have the ability to choose whether you're fearful or optimistic, for both fear and optimism are decisions you make.

Remember the law firm I worked with in San Francisco, where I was asked to "do something" with the angry manager of the Los Angeles office? They are a great example of this distinction. The firm had grown rapidly and extensively from its beginnings in 1975 up to and through 1990. Then, something happened, and the growth suddenly stopped. When I was contacted in 1996, it was on the verge of a decline.

The management team was leaving for a strategic planning retreat to plot a course to get them back on track, and they contacted me to facilitate the retreat. When I agreed, the first

thing I insisted on doing was to interview as many of the partners as possible who were at the firm since the beginning so I
could find out what the problem was.

What I learned was truly fascinating. Everyone told me that
during the growth years, the firm's "leader" (whom I'll call
Larry), was the most optimistic, the most positive, the most
encouraging person you could ever imagine meeting. His philosophy was to have fun, do good work, take care of the clients, and let success take care of itself. The firm never did any
marketing; they just did what Larry said. They had lots of fun,
they did the best job they could do for their clients, and most
important, they never worried. Why? Because Larry told them
not to.

One of the firm's partners (whom I'll call Paul), told me a
particularly telling story. The firm specialized in litigating
very large cases, and it wasn't atypical for a team of lawyers to
work on a single case full-time. Paul was part of a team of five
lawyers who had worked for several years on one multi-mil-
lion dollar case. One day the case settled, leaving the five lawyers with no work and with no obvious source of new work.

So Paul went to Larry and asked, "What do we do now?"

As was typical for Larry, his response was, "Don't worry
about it. You five have been working hard for a number of
years. You've earned a break. Tell your team to take some
time off and have fun. I guarantee you it won't take long
before we'll be screaming to get you back here."

That wasn't what Paul expected to hear because he was
worried they'd all be laid off. But Paul was a young attorney,
and if Larry said not to worry, who was he to do otherwise? So

Paul and his team took off. Less than thirty days later, a new case came in, and Paul and his team were back at it.

I heard story after story that replicated Paul's. The mood of the firm was one of faith, trust, and optimism, because that's the kind of leader Larry was. As a result, the firm grew and grew and grew. It's a great example of the law of cause and effect operating in all its glory.

So what happened? Well, one day in 1990, Larry woke up and looked at what he had created. He had hundreds of people working in the firm, with a payroll in the tens of millions of dollars. Stated simply, he got scared. He related to the group and me at this strategic planning retreat that up until that fateful day he was confident of their ability to thrive. But for some reason, on that day, he awoke and said, "Oh my God. We have most of our work coming from one client. They have been able to send us big cases for 15 years, but can it really continue?" He started to doubt. Fear set in. And the rest got ugly.

The day after that realization, Larry gathered his partners around the conference table and expressed his concerns. He said that they had to market, diversify, and look for new clients; it wasn't good that they had all their eggs in one basket. Unfortunately, Larry's partners didn't know what to make of this. They didn't want to market. They never had and didn't know how. Everyone had a different opinion about what they should do. They started to argue, bicker, and make each other wrong. The teamwork went out the window, taking all the wind out of their sails. In the face of their confusion, the results turned to confusion.

Happily, this story has a wonderful ending. We got what happened out on the table during the strategic planning retreat. We followed it up with several multi-day partner retreats to "clean up" all the upsets, disappointments, and frustrations that occurred during those six rocky years. In the end, everyone committed to get back to "what brung them:" having fun, taking care of the clients, doing good work, and being optimistic about the future. The last I heard, the firm was breaking growth records.

## Scarcity

People are afraid of many things: death, public speaking, failure, success, embarrassment, the list goes on and on. One fear, in particular, is so prevalent in our culture yet so unrecognized that it needs special attention. It's a fear that is passed down from generation to generation in a very subtle way.

In speeches and workshops, I frequently ask the attendees: "When you were a child, did your parents tell you to eat all of the food on your plate because there were poor people starving somewhere?" I know my parents told me this. I suspect yours did too. But until I started asking the question, I had no idea that almost everyone received this message. In my programs, almost everyone responds with a "yes." It's often fun to find out where their parents told them the starving people lived. It's usually China or Africa, but sometimes other exotic places.

When you stop to think about it, though, it's bizarre to say that you have to eat all your food because somebody is starving in some far off land. How is your eating your food (or not) going to impact this starving person? Regardless, this is what we hear, and there is a powerful message hidden in these words. The obvious message is that you don't want to waste food. However, what goes along with that is the implication that you don't want to waste food because our planet's resources are limited/finite. Thus, we develop a belief in scarcity. And whenever we have a belief in scarcity, we have a corresponding fear that we won't have enough or that what we have will get used up.

Look at our culture and look into your own life to see if you experience this. Aren't we told that the American game is to work hard, invest, plan for the future, save, and accumulate, and don't you spend time doing just that? Don't businesses spend an inordinate amount of time doing strategic planning? Aren't most people investing, gambling, playing the stock market, buying lottery tickets, or trying something to get or accumulate as much money as possible?

Now you might question, "What's wrong with that?" Well, nothing is *wrong* at all. But if you or your company are saving and investing simply because you are coming from a belief in scarcity – a fear that if you don't, either the money will run out or you won't have enough – then there are serious consequences.

When you come from scarcity, money becomes very important. You believe that one day you'll have enough and you'll feel secure. But it never happens. Remember, you can't get to anyplace other than where you start. So if the underlying belief is scarcity, no matter how much you have, it's never enough. No amount of money is ever enough in a paradigm of scarcity. The more you get, the more you want. It's an endless game. You end up being in the game for the money, and you end up appearing or actually being greedy.

The events of 2002 are evidence of this. Think about Enron, MCI, and Adelphia Cable. These companies had fortunes, but it wasn't enough to satisfy the key officers. Rampant greed took over. Now I ask you, once you're a multi-millionaire, how much more do you need? Tens of thousands of people die every day from starvation while corporate executives in the United States earn tens of millions of dollars yearly. While I have no problem with people earning whatever is fair, the paychecks of some executives have clearly gotten way out of proportion. And it's all driven by this paradigm we live in – a paradigm of fear and scarcity.

When you come from scarcity, guess what you attract into your life? Scarcity! This is why the majority of people struggle to make ends meet, often not even accomplishing that.

And when you come from both fear and scarcity, guess what you experience in life? Struggle, effort, stress, sleepless nights, depression, you name it. You simply can't have happiness or satisfaction in that pattern of thinking.

So many people think they'll one day get to abundance. But you can't get to abundance with scarcity thinking. Scarcity thinking is useful for one and only one thing: producing scarcity.

## Chapter 8

# You and Your Company

WE HAVE enough cards on the table now, so we can pause for a few moments and take the opportunity to reflect on what we've discussed. Doing so will lay the foundation for where we go next.

Where we will continue to go is deeper and deeper into the paradigm we are all living in. At each stop along the way, it's quite helpful to reflect on what you are uncovering about yourself and your company.

I want to ask you several questions. Consider each in turn and take some time to either write or reflect on your answers:

- What do you see so far about you? Your company?
- Where are you personally?
- Where do you think your company is?

As you think about the answers to these questions, consider such aspects as happiness, satisfaction, who people are for you, the quality of your relationships, etc.

Realize that nobody lives totally in fear or totally in trust, faith, and optimism, just as nobody lives totally in scarcity or

totally in abundance. So if you create two continuums, one
with fear at 0 and trust/faith/optimism at 100, and the other
with scarcity at 0 and abundance at 100, what score would you
give yourself on each? What score would you give your company? How do you think others in your company would score
the organization? Ask them. You might learn something about
other people's attitudes or about the mood of the company.

If you didn't give yourself a score of 100 on the fear/opti-
mism continuum, answer these questions:

- What are you worrying about?
- What happened that initiated that worry?
- What impact does that or those concerns have on your
  peace of mind?
- Is whatever there is in your conversation regarding the
  world being a scary and/or limited place necessary? Really?
- Is it necessary that you be where you are on the
  continuums?
- More important, is this thinking useful? Helpful?

After you've answered these questions, and it's important
to answer them honestly before moving on, consider the
following:

You are where you are because that's where you've chosen
to be. You likely chose sometime long ago, maybe when you
were three or four or five years old, maybe based on some attitude or comment your mother or father made. And today
you live with that choice, without ever re-examining it.

## How We Choose Our Messages

When I was very young, I lived in New York City. When I was old enough to go outside and play with my friends on my own, my mother would always say as I was walking out the door, "Be careful!" She didn't say, "I love you," "Have a great time," or "Have fun," but "Be careful." I didn't know at the time that was her code for all of the other statements I just listed. But I do know the impact it had on me. I concluded there must be something I had to be careful about! And of course there were other prescriptions like "Don't talk to strangers." I can see in hindsight that it was then I learned there were things/people to be afraid of.

Then there was also the "eat all the food on your plate" message, which introduced me to the idea of scarcity. So I lived most of my life at the low ends of both the fear/optimism and scarcity/abundance continuums. At some level, that's what I chose. At another level, that's what chose me! But those were the choices that used my life.

The great part of being an adult and fully understanding what we have been discussing so far is the realization that you can always choose again. And again. And again. You're not stuck with the choices you've made in the past, unless you choose to do that. Many reasons exist as to why people choose to stay in their old belief systems, and we'll get to them later. But I suggest that life is a choice, and your job, especially as a leader in the new paradigm we are creating, is to choose wisely.

In other words, you can see the glass as either half empty or half full, and your choice makes all the difference in the world. You may have heard this said before, but I want to give it new meaning for you. If you're always seeing what's missing, what you will attract into your life is more of the missing. That's the law of cause and effect in action. But if you always see what's there, if you are grateful and appreciative for what you have rather than complaining about what you don't have, you'll attract into your life more to be grateful for.

Consider the possibility that the amount of abundance in your life is exactly consistent with your willingness to think abundantly and that what materializes in your physical world is simply an out-picturing of what's going on in your internal world.

Too many people think the way to create more abundance is to work harder. Nonsense! Plenty of people work very hard and have very little, just as others hardly work and have a lot. And it's not about luck or working smart. You create abundance with your thinking. Do you want to be abundant? Think abundantly. Do you want to be poor? Believe in scarcity.

## Pay Attention to Your Mood

How does all of this apply on an organizational level? How do you use this information to make work work? An organization is a collection of thinking beings. As a result, it has a collective energy – a mood – that determines what's possible.

If the mood is upbeat, enthusiastic, positive, and optimistic, and people are all pulling together, you're going to have great results. Remember the San Francisco law firm I worked with? The mood during those fifteen growth years was extraordinary. And so were their results.

But if people are fearful, selfish, coming from scarcity, not working together, then watch out. This is a formula for disaster.

Many years ago a Los Angeles company hired me to coach them. The company was not doing well. As usual, I spent a day at the company and interviewed as many people as possible. What I found was almost scary. The company president/owner thought that fear was a great motivator, so he used it regularly. During the weekly staff meetings, he would spend most of the time telling people how terrible things were, how bad the shape the company was in, and how uncertain the financial outlook was. Then he would end by saying that if they all didn't get to work and produce some results, he couldn't be sure he could keep the doors open.

He thought that approach would motivate them to work harder. One staff member revealed that she would often go home so depressed that she would drink herself to sleep. People were afraid all the time. And, interestingly, fear did motivate them. But it created a mood of gloom and doom, and these words adequately describe their results.

At the end of the interviews, I discussed my findings with the president. Because he felt that fear was a great motivator for him, he assumed it would be a great motivator for others. But he didn't consider the negative impact it had on the employees' mood. Ultimately, he agreed to change his ways, and the results started to change soon thereafter.

## Set The Right Tone

Again, pause and ask yourself . . .

- What's the truth about your organization?
- Is that truth what you're committed to?
- Where do you need to go from here?

➤ How do you create the kind of company that makes you happy and proud, and that produces extraordinary results?

As the leader of your organization, you set the company's tone. If you're excited, enthusiastic, optimistic, and positive, your people will follow suit. Conversely, if you motivate with fear and are negative and pessimistic, your people will be that way too. Being a leader means being conscious of the tone you set.

Setting the right tone is all a matter of where you start. Start from where you want to end up. Start from being a happy group of satisfied, turned on, joyous, alive, enthusiastic, optimistic people, having faith in the future, working together, aligned on a vision, with a commitment to support each other in being that way, and watch out. Nothing and nobody will be able to interfere with your success.

## Chapter 9

# Listening in the Existing Paradigm

BOOKS AND courses abound on "active" listening and other so-called effective listening techniques. But I ask you: have any of those ideas really made a difference? While they have probably helped a little, as a "technique," they have their limitations. So let's examine listening in a new way – a way that *will* make an enormous and permanent impact on your life.

Typically we speak to people as if they were a blank canvas upon which we can write words that they will receive and understand exactly as we intend. And, when they don't "get" our message exactly as we intend, we get irritated and think they must not be listening, don't understand, are playing games, or are being hostile. The list goes on and on.

But given everything we've said so far, are we really speaking to a blank canvas? Of course not. The other person is living in his or her conversation. Before you even open your mouth, he is already listening, to *himself*. Why? Because people are *always* listening to their own internal conversation.

In workshops and speeches, I often ask the audience, "Has anyone ever asked you: Are you listening to me?" A laugh of recognition usually follows, because we've all probably been asked that same question. I then ask, "What's the only honest answer you can give someone if she asks that?" The answer of course is, "No, I'm not listening to you; I'm listening to me listening to you!"

So the question is not *whether* we are listening when someone speaks to us; rather, it's a question of *how* we are listening. We always have a conversation going on within us as we listen to another, and that conversation filters and determines everything we hear. As a result of many years of looking at this subject and participating in enumerable programs, I have come to realize that people listen in one or more of a number of ways. Try to identify the way *you* listen as we go through some of the more common ones.

### ❧ Get to the Point

When I first began to pay attention to how I listened, (that is, listening to my internal conversation when people spoke to me), I realized that my predominant way of listening was what I will call *get to the point*. I was always busy, doing something, and very much focused on what *I* was doing and the importance *I* assigned to it. In my mind, people, like secretaries, vendors, friends, children, my spouse, were always interfering with whatever *I* happened to be doing at the moment. Couldn't they see I was busy? I wanted them to get to the point quickly so I could get back to what I was doing.

As they'd talk to me, internally I would be saying, "What's this all about? Why are you telling me this? Can't you see I'm busy? Would you please hurry up and get to the point!" In fact, it would often be so bad that if they didn't *get to the point* quickly, I would usually say something like, "Would you please tell me the point of all this."

Many years after the fact I finally understood why I had so much trouble keeping a secretary for the fifteen years I was in private law practice. Instead of treating my secretary as a valued ally, I treated her as an interruption to something more important that I had to do.

Can you relate to this way of listening? In almost every group I speak to, when I ask how many people in the audience listen *get to the point,* most of the hands go up. Perhaps this is a result of our fast-paced society, where everyone is working so hard to overcome his or her fears and sense of scarcity and trying to stay one step ahead of the bill collectors.

## ❧ Do I Agree?

Another common way people listen is to determine if they agree or disagree with what you are saying. A variation of this is when people listen to determine whether you are speaking the truth. So you'll be talking to someone and he or she will say, "Yes, I agree with that (or I believe that)," or "No, I don't agree with that, nor that, but yes, I agree with that . . ." And so forth.

These people know what they know, believe what they believe, and then listen to see if what you are speaking fits or doesn't fit into their existing belief system. If it does, you're obviously very wise, as wise as them, and they acknowledge you for that. If it doesn't, you're obviously ignorant or uninformed, and they proudly let you know that. Strike any chords?

## ✺ What Am I Going to Say Next?

I have lots of relatives who listen in a way that I call *what am I going to say next*. People who listen this way like (or rather, need) to do all the talking. In fact, they think that's the way you win friends and influence people. *Talk, talk more, talk a lot* is their motto. They want people to "get" how brilliant they are.

So when someone else is speaking, they're just listening to get ammunition for what they are going to talk about next. And, when they get their cue, they typically interrupt you mid-sentence and go on their merry way. Or, they wait patiently for you to stop talking so they can have their turn. Does this sound like anyone you know? Yourself maybe?

Sometimes I have to laugh at the conversations I have with my mom. *She'll* ask *me* a question, like how's the weather in California (where I live – she lives in Florida), and I'll start to answer. In the middle of my sentence, she'll pick up on a word I use to describe our weather (which relates to her weather), and start to tell me about the weather in Florida. It's like she never asked me anything at all. Have you ever had this happen to you, or have you ever done this to another?

## ✺ Let Me Tell You What You are About to Say

A slight variation of the previous way of listening is people who listen with the goal of *figuring out* what you're going to say next. After all, they know you, they've heard you talk before, they're sure they know where you're going with this, and to show how smart they are (or because they don't have the patience to let you finish) they finish whatever you are speaking about for you. It's like they're playing a game called *let me figure out what you are going to say and tell you.*

## ❧ I'm Always Right

Some people think, and actually believe, that there is a *right* way to do *everything* and, conversely, a *wrong* way to do everything. And guess who knows the right way to do everything? You guessed it – they do! While they don't say or admit this, they do *everything* the *right* way. That's what makes it the right way; it's their way.

These folks also constantly compare what you are doing to the *right* way of doing things. And, as you would expect, they are very good at telling you that your way is the *wrong* way.

People who listen this way often startle me. They seem to have no perception that everyone has a unique way of doing things, that there is no *right* or *wrong* way, and that everything is just a matter of opinion and preference. They truly believe there is just one way of doing everything – the right way, which is *their* way.

Shortly after I moved to my new beach apartment in Southern California, I decided to invite some friends and relatives over for a party. I provided some of the food and invited people to bring snacks to share as well as whatever they liked to drink. When people arrived, we put all the food, snacks, and drinks on a buffet style table. I provided plates and glasses and ice. My guests helped themselves to the food and drink, allowing me to mingle and enjoy the party with everyone else.

When my sister arrived at the party, it didn't take long for her to lecture me that "you just don't do that at a party." She proceeded to explain that when "you" have a party it's "your" responsibility to provide the food and the beverages. If anyone wants to bring anything, that's up to them, not you. It's also "your" responsibility to pour the drinks and make sure everyone always has whatever they need. There was more to the instructions she gave me, but by now I forget.

Thus started a long history of my sister explaining to me, at just about every opportunity, how things are "supposed" to be done and how inappropriate I was for doing things the "wrong" way. Do you know anybody like that?

### I Need to Win

An offshoot of *I'm always right* is when people turn every conversation into a debate. As soon as you start a conversation with a *debate* person, you can feel the energy shift. They go on the offensive. This way of listening is not so much about being right or wrong, it's about winning. These people will argue and argue and argue and argue, until you either give up or admit that they've won.

### Attack

I have met many people who, especially in close, intimate relationships, listen as if they are being *attacked*. For whatever reason (the reasons for all of these ways of listening will get clear before long), they fear you are out to get them, to make them wrong, to take advantage of them, etc. They are on guard, on the defensive, and whatever you say, they respond as if you just attacked them.

Very often, it's the most casual of comments, the slightest criticism, the off-hand remark that they rebut with a surprisingly hostile response, as if you had just intentionally stuck a knife in their heart. I'm always caught off-guard when someone responds this way. I can't imagine how they could have heard what I said in a way that prompted such a response.

## ❧ Black Hat

Of course, no list like this would be complete without mentioning the people who, no matter what the idea or possibility, tell you why it *won't* work. These are the *black hat* listeners. They've seen and tried everything. They've been there, done that; they know that there is some reason why every idea won't work; and it's their goal to tell you precisely what the reason is. They listen for the flaw in your plan and then leap to your rescue.

## ❧ I Know

Some people listen *I know*. These people know everything. Just ask them! Whatever you say, they say, "I know." If you ask them how they know, they say, "I just know."

## ❧ Either/Or

Another common way of listening, which is usually not *instead* of but *in addition* to these other ways, is called *either/or*. This way of listening stems from childhood. Remember being told when you were young that you can't have your cake and eat it too? This message told you that life is about choices. As a result, some people believe that everything has to be one way or another, and they listen to hear the choices. They believe that sooner or later, everything comes down to a compromise or a choice.

## Are You Approving of Me?

Although I suspect you could probably add more to this list, the final group of people listen simply to determine whether the speaker is approving or disapproving of them. People who listen this way are fundamentally insecure about their own self worth. Rather than resolving it within themselves, they look to others for their validation. So the whole focus of their listening is to see if they are being approved of or not.

## Back to You

Keeping with the methodology of this book, re-examine the above ways that people listen. Map it onto your experience. Can you identify the predominant way that you listen? What about the other people in your life? Your spouse, your children, some of your key executives and employees? Next time you speak to any of these people, or to anyone for that matter, listen to how they respond. Listen to what comes out of their mouth. Try to identify the way they listen. With some practice, you'll be able to do this easily. This exercise will certainly help you understand the world they live in and why they react to things the way they do.

Now that you've identified the primary way you listen, consider the possibility that at different times you listen in most if not all of the ways described above. Can you see that this is the case? At this point, it is helpful to tell the truth about how you listen.

That then brings us to the next question: Do you decide in advance how you are going to listen? That is, do you decide in advance that when you walk in the office in the morning you're going to listen *do I agree?*, and then at 10 a.m., in the sales meeting, you're going to switch to *get to the point?* Likely not, correct? Likely, you just listen how you listen without any thought about it. In fact, when I ask people at a speech or in a seminar, "How many of you decide in advance how you are going to listen?" I always get a laugh as the predominant response. Think about how I'm going to listen in advance? It seems ridiculous.

These ways of listening are unconscious and automatic. Our conversation is what it is; it has a mind of its own. Therefore, we listen how we listen, we react to the things we react to without much if any forethought, and it just is that way.

Also consider that people, you and I, aren't aware of the power of our listening. We go through life like a victim, like someone is doing it to us. I say, no. There is no such thing as a victim. We shape our world with how we listen. If we listen *attack*, guess how everything shows up for us? Like an attack! If we listen *do I agree?*, then that's what's available to us in any discussion. You get no new information, no new ideas, and no ability for anyone to make a difference with you. All you get to do is agree or disagree.

Do you know people who are skeptical? Consider that there is no such "thing" as being skeptical. You can show me a table or a chair or a tomato, but can you show me skepticism? No. It's just a way of listening.

Skepticism is an internal conversation that goes something like this: "I know that many things (maybe most things) are

BS, a rip-off, not what they appear to be. This probably is too, and you can't fool me!" So it's a way of listening to defend yourself against being made to look foolish.

We can have the same discussion about resignation. Can you show me resignation? No. It's a way of listening. It's a conversation that "nothing will change; this won't make a difference; it hasn't worked in the past, so it certainly won't now."

It's all unconscious. And these are the ways people listen.

## The Pattern in the Process

Who do you have your attention on when you listen in *any* of the previously described ways? Obviously yourself!

Now the really important question is: What do you think this type of listening is designed for? In other words, if you were to design human beings and have them listen in the ways listed above, what do you think the underlying purpose would be? Please take a moment, go back over the list, and see if you can identify the pattern, the design.

ঌ

If you did the exercise, you'll realize that in *all* of these ways of listening, you have your attention on yourself, and your only concern is your own self-interest. You could say that you are concerned with protecting yourself, because each of these ways of listening is fundamentally adversarial in nature. You're over there; I'm over here. You show up as a threat to me and I have to protect myself from you.

Why can't we all just get along? In most interactions, at least interactions in the existing paradigm, we have person A with his attention on himself and concerned with his own self-interests, and person B with her attention on herself and concerned with protecting herself. When they talk to each other, do they have a meaningful, intimate conversation? No way. Most conversations resemble two television sets tuned to different channels, broadcasting at each other.

This is why we rarely experience true communication between people. Each person's primary concern is his or her own self-interest and desire to make sure the other person hears what he or she has to say. But people place very little or no attention on making sure they understand the other person. This is the root cause of most miscommunications and upsets between spouses, parents and children, team members, and bosses and employees. It certainly is my experience given the number of companies I've worked with.

In addition to waking up to and becoming conscious of your listening, you also need to understand that when you listen in any of these ways, your end-product is precisely what these ways of listening are designed for ... your survival. If that's what you want, then go ahead and listen that way. Just recognize that like everything else in life, there are consequences for everything you do and every way you are.

Here are some of the consequences of having your attention on yourself and listening in one or more of the previous ways: There is no real communication, no understanding, no appreciation of the other person's position, no intimacy, and certainly no trust. These consequences cost you your satisfaction, happiness, sense of well being, self-confidence, joy, aliveness, and ultimately the relationship. In a business setting, it costs productivity, creativity, teamwork, enthusiasm, turnover, success, and of course, money, results, and accomplishment.

Is it any wonder why our companies, our relationships, and our world are the way they are? Is it any wonder why communication doesn't work and why our relationships suffer? We'll talk more in Chapter 11 about why we are this way, but for now, let's simply recognize the impact our listening has on our relationships and our lives. And we can better understand all of the ways of listening discussed when we look at them as being self-protection strategies . . . and when we remember that it's just a conversation.

*Chapter 10*

# A New Way of Listening

ONCE YOU become aware of *how* you listen, which simply means becoming conscious of where you have your attention and your internal dialog when others are speaking to you, you can choose to *not* listen that way any longer. Initially, this shift will take focus, commitment, and staying conscious, but with a bit of practice, you can train yourself to generate a different way of listening. Why would you want to do that? To avoid the severe consequences associated with the ways of listening discussed in the previous chapter.

The first step is obvious. Since when we listen unconsciously we have our attention on ourselves, to generate a more constructive way of listening you need to put your attention on the other person. That part is simple. The tougher question is: What do you listen *for*?

Let me suggest a few ways of listening to get the discussion started. You're sure to think of others as we go.

## ❧ Possibility

Would you like to learn how to totally suppress the creativity of the people around you? When they come to you with an idea that they are excited about, listen "get to the point," "find the flaw," "what am I going to say next," "right/wrong," etc. Of course you don't want to do that even though in the past you may have done exactly that unconsciously.

So would you now like to learn how to encourage people's creativity? Listen for *possibility*. In other words, suppose someone is speaking to you about an idea he has. Instead of thinking about whether you like the idea, or whether you think it would work, or whether you agree with it, etc., put your attention on him and ask yourself, "What's possible in this idea?" Manage your internal conversation to be inquisitive, to speculate with him, to be influenced by what he is saying. See if you can match his enthusiasm. Ask questions. Get into his reality. Work hard to see what he sees. You don't have to like it or agree with it. Just see the possibility.

This way of listening is very desirable for an executive because it *encourages* creativity in the workplace. Most leaders certainly want their staff to be creative. So if a staff member comes up with an idea and you determine that you don't have time to listen, or that "we've done that before," or that it won't work, or any of the other automatic ways of listening, then don't be surprised if that's the last idea you hear from him.

But if you get honestly enthusiastic about his idea and see it through as far as you can, he will be encouraged to create something else, even if you don't implement the initial idea. So listening for possibility is definitely a recommended way to listen.

### Commitment

Think of the last time someone came to you with a complaint. If you're like most people, you had your attention on yourself and were concerned with your survival. As you communicated with the complainer, your internal dialog probably went something like this: "Please, leave me alone. Can't you see I'm busy?" or "Here he comes again. How can I get rid of him this time so I can get back to what I have to do?"

I recently asked a group of speech attendees what some of their reactions are when they see a complaint coming. The answers were actually quite amusing. Things they would do were close their door, get on the phone, leave, hide, go to the restroom, and other things like that.

Consider the possibility that in most cases, people complain to their boss because something isn't working and it's important to them that it work. In other words, the thing that isn't working is getting in the way of something they are committed to. The fact that this is often the case may not be obvious, but I assert that's because you haven't listened for the other person's commitment.

This brings us to the next desirable way of listening – *listening for people's commitment*. Get your attention off yourself, get it on the speaker, and manage your conversation to be listening for what he or she is committed to.

I helped facilitate to resolution a situation in an office between two secretaries that illustrate this way of listening. One secretary, Shirley, kept finding Sally's papers in, around, and on top of the copy machine every time she went to make a copy. And it really bothered her. So she went to the office manager, Lois, to complain. As this had happened before, Lois was tired of her complaining and asked me what to do.

I told her that the next time Shirley came to her, she should listen for her commitment and tell Shirley what she heard. Here's how it eventually played out. Shirley walked into Lois's office, now really upset, and said, "This is getting out of hand. Sally's papers are all over the copy machine, and I can't get anything done."

Lois replied, "Let me understand this. What I hear is that you are committed to getting your work done in a timely and efficient manner, and when Sally leaves her papers around the copy machine, that gets in the way of your commitment."

Shirley stopped in her tracks (as will happen every time people have the experience of being heard). Lois reported that Shirley's upset suddenly disappeared. Rather than continuing to complain, Shirley looked at Lois and said, "Yes, that's exactly right."

If you listen for someone's commitment and tell her what you hear, only two outcomes are possible. Either you'll get it right or you won't. But either way, you win. If you get it right, she will respond as Shirley did. If you don't, she'll likely say something like, "No, that's not what I'm committed to. What I'm committed to is . . ."

Returning to Shirley and Lois, Lois then said, "Good, I thought so. And I acknowledge you for your commitment to be a great secretary. Let's talk to Sally and find out what's going on with her and what she's committed to that prompts her to leave her papers all over the copy machine."

By handling the situation the way she did, Lois took the circumstances out of the realm of right/wrong and good/bad, which is where most differences play out and why it's normally so difficult to reach resolution. Second, the phrase "all over the copy machine" is a judgment, not the truth. In confronting Sally, Lois needed to take that judgment out of the equation or Sally would feel wronged. There is no peace in a context of right/wrong. More about that later.

So Shirley and Lois went to pay Sally a visit. As coached, Lois addressed Sally by saying, "Shirley has been finding it difficult to get her work done as efficiently as she would like because of the delays she's experiencing when she has to make copies. Apparently, when she gets to the copy machine, she frequently finds your papers in the feeder or still in the sorter, and she has to remove them and find you before she can make her copies. (Notice, she stuck to the facts rather than being accusatory and using words like "you leave your papers all over the copy machine.") So, we're wondering what you're committed to that has this situation occur." (Notice further that rather than being made wrong, Sally is actually being acknowledged. That makes it easy for her to tell the truth.)

Sally's answer was predictable. She wasn't a slob, careless, or inconsiderate, all of which are judgments Shirley could have easily come to. Rather, she said, "I'm doing work right now for four people. They have me running like crazy. And frankly, I'm overwhelmed. I'm in the middle of a job for one person, and one of the others comes and grabs me to do something for her. Or I'm in the middle of a job, and I go back to my desk to get something I need, and one of them corners me. I'm really, really sorry. I can imagine what an upset this must be for you Shirley, but I don't mean to do it, and I just don't know what to do."

At this point, many possible solutions exist, and it doesn't matter how it gets resolved. What's important is that Shirley and Lois now have some understanding and compassion for Sally's situation, and I guarantee you they'll work it out. In fact, what actually happened was that Shirley apologized to Sally for being so insensitive and volunteered to help her get her work done. They became great friends and teammates instead of adversaries. And it all happened because Lois, rather than shutting Shirley down, which we all too frequently do when someone complains, listened for her commitment.

## Go For the Gold

Since your focus and your conversation determine the way you listen, another possible way of listening you could generate is *listening for the gold*. I named this style after the story I told you back in Chapter 6 when I was working with my colleague Rita. If you recall, she told me that she sees a bar of solid gold in everyone.

Since listening and speaking ultimately are the opposite sides of the same coin, you could either generate that all people are brilliant, gorgeous, talented, and fabulous in your conversation and/or you could be listening for the brilliance, beauty, talent, and fabulousness when someone is speaking to you. Either way, it's going to be an awesome listening experience for anyone you talk to.

## Compassion

I'm wondering if you are one of the rare people who never get upset? Not very likely. Trying to live your life not getting upset can be very upsetting. Human beings get upset; that's a fact. What's not so obvious is that upsets are almost always irrational. It's my understanding of human nature that we develop an upset mechanism when we are very young and that this mechanism stays with us for the rest of our lives. Whenever something or somebody triggers the mechanism, we get upset. Now we know what triggered the mechanism and so we *think* that is the cause of the upset (usually the person that pushed our button), but that is simply not the case. The upset is an illogical, built-in reaction to some event or circumstance.

I also recently asked a group of speech attendees what they often say when people around them get upset. I loved the answers. Here's what they say: "chill out," "what are you getting so upset about?" "it will be OK," "relax," "take a Valium," "get over it," and "give it a break!"

Please, don't ever say any of those things. When people are upset, they need a safe place to communicate their feelings. If you are willing to provide that, the upset can go away. How do you do that? *Listen with compassion.*

I first heard this discussed in 1989 when I was invited to join the Lew Epstein International Men's Club. Lew and his wife Francine had men's and women's clubs all around the country, and one in London, and each month they would travel from city to city, meeting with groups of men and women.

The objective of the clubs was to provide a safe place for men and women to deal with the issues they faced in their relationships. In one of my earliest meetings, I remember Lew talking about us listening to each other with compassion, which he said was listening with a deep appreciation of *the other person's* feelings and experience. It's not listening to see how *you* feel or think about what the other person is saying, but how the other person feels about what he or she is saying.

In the years I was in the Club, I learned that in a conversation with another person, especially when they were upset, I could turn off my internal conversation and stop the constant judging of what the other person was saying. I could literally "get over there" with him, focus on what's going on with him, and actually re-create what he was feeling and experiencing.

Lew was the master of this. In the thirteen years I knew Lew, I never experienced him judging me or anyone else. When you were with Lew, he was with you, there for you, listening with all the empathy and compassion you can imagine. He was a true gift to us men and women, as we always knew that we were "safe" in his presence. He would not judge us, he wouldn't make us wrong, he wouldn't even have an opinion about what we were doing or whom we were being. The result was that we could talk to him about anything, and we were always confident that he wouldn't use it against us. What an incredible gift he was to all of us!

But what Lew did for us is not the point. The point is that you can do this too. You can be for your staff, your employees, your customers, your spouse, your children, and your friends who Lew was for us. You can make it safe for the people in your life to talk to you and tell you what's on their mind. You can provide a safe space for them to resolve their upsets. You can have them feel like you're there for them and give them an experience of being heard. Just listen for the gold and listen with compassion. That's it. Nothing else is required. But as Lew would say, "It's simple, not easy." It is simple, but it will take daily practice and a huge commitment on your part to master this if you are going to reap the rewards that come along with this way of listening.

And one last thing. When you are upset, be very careful what comes out of your mouth. Remember, it's irrational. You think you know why you're upset, but you really don't. Don't attack; don't lash out. Lew used to tell us to just say: "I'm upset, I'm really upset." Keep it simple. Find a person who will listen to your upset with compassion so you can let it go.

## ❧ Win/Win

Another very powerful way to listen in business is *win/win*. Instead of listening to see if you are going to win, without much attention on whether the other person wins (which, quite frankly, is what you find most of the time in business), you put your attention on the other person and find ways for him to win in the transaction too.

I coached a company president, Joe, for many years as he grew his business steadily year after year. Working with Joe was a great joy because he took this way of listening to the next step. His listening was what he called *win/win/win*. As they developed new products, new packaging, new advertising, whatever, he would always ask, "How is the company going to win, how are all our employees and stakeholders going to win, and how is the customer going to win." People in the company learned quickly that you had better figure all of that out before presenting something to Joe. His commitment was that everyone wins.

I'm not asserting that Joe's way is the "right" way to listen in running a company, but it sure seemed then and sure seems now to be a "smart" way. It's been my experience that you can only play the win/lose game for so long. Sooner or later, people are going to be on to you. And that doesn't even address the fact that you have to be able to sleep at night. History has proven that companies that operate from the perspective of everybody winning, including the environment, the community, the nation, everybody, come out ahead in the long run.

## ❧ And/Both

The final way of listening I want to suggest is what I call *and/both*. In the unconscious ways of listening we had *either/or*, as in "You can't have your cake and eat it too," or "It's either going to be this way or that way." With *either/or*, somebody wins and somebody loses. Somebody has to compromise.

Who says? Maybe it doesn't have to be that way. After all, it's just a conversation in the existing paradigm. And, like all of the other conversations, we're not stuck with it. So I'm suggesting listening to determine ways that you don't have to choose, that nobody has to compromise, that you can both/all have it your way, and that you get to have your cake and eat it too. Will you always be able to figure out a way "to have it all?" Sometimes yes and sometimes no. But why not try? You have everything to gain and nothing to lose.

### The Listening Advantage

You could certainly generate other ways of listening, but *listening for possibility, listening for commitment, listening for the gold, listening with compassion, listening win/win,* and *listening and/both* are my favorites. In all of these ways, you have your attention on the other person as you manage your conversation.

What are the advantages of listening in one or more of these ways? Recall the list of consequences you experience when you listen with your attention on yourself and in one of the unconscious ways. All of those consequences now become what's available to you with this new way of listening.

That is, there is real communication, understanding, appreciation of the other person's position, intimacy, and certainly trust. And what that makes available is satisfaction, happiness, a sense of well being, self-confidence, joy, aliveness, and ultimately rich, meaningful, quality relationships. In a business setting, the payoff is productivity, creativity, teamwork, enthusiasm, no turnover, success and of course, money, results, and accomplishment. You get all of this just by switching the way you listen. And remember, your listening is just a conversation.

What do you have to give up to get these benefits? Well, the need to be right, to win, to have it your way, to focus on yourself to the exclusion of others, etc. These aren't things humans find easy to give up. But it's a worthy trade, I assert, and one I invite you to take on.

*Sometimes if both people are willing to listen carefully,
it is possible to do more than exchange greetings
and good wishes. Even to do more than exchange
information. The two people may even find out
something which neither of them knew before.*

&#42; Gregory Bateson

*Chapter 11*

# The Design of Life

BEFORE WE continue, let me assure you that this book is not intended in any way to be a psychological treatise. After all, I'm a coach, not a psychologist. Having said that, the discussion herein would be incomplete without some mention of why we are the way we are, and more particularly, why we have our attention on ourselves and are concerned with our survival.

If you recall, we discussed in Chapter 3 the origins of "the conversation." Reviewing the salient points, we said that when we are born, for all practical purposes, there is no conversation. But it doesn't stay that way for long. All kinds of events occur. Our diaper is wet and we cry. Someone comes right away or doesn't. At any given time, any one of a number of people is around us doing something. Mothers, fathers, sisters, brothers, grandparents . . . the list goes on and on.

Soon we grow, mature, and develop a personality. We crawl; we walk; we talk; people react to what we do. We go to school and interact with other children and teachers. The number of events we experience is endless.

In reality, none of these events inherently mean anything. But human beings have a hard time believing that events don't mean anything. In fact, we believe just the opposite. We think *everything* means *something*.

So, beginning at an early age, we start interpreting everything that occurs and assigning it a meaning. And it's important to understand that for us, the event does indeed have the meaning we give it, whether fact or not. For us, it is "true."

Then we store the event, with the meaning we gave it, in our consciousness. Of course, it doesn't stop there. The next event occurs, we interpret it, give it some meaning, and store it away. We repeat the process again and again and again. Along the way, we make judgments and decisions about ourselves, the world, other people, and how we fit in. What emerges is an elaborate story about everything. The entire process – the decisions, the judgments, the story – are all a part of our conversation.

## How This Process Shapes Who We Are

Now let's add to that process the paradigm in which we were born. In that paradigm, there were and are parents, grandparents, relatives, friends, teachers, and the like. I will call that group "adults." What's apparent but not said is that the adults are the ones who *know*. They are the smart ones. They are the ones who have the experience, so they know! And, of course, the children are the ones who *don't know*. Therein lies the major part of the problem. As children, we were treated like we didn't know, and it didn't take us long to figure that out.

So the adults' job is to teach the children. Unfortunately, very few of our parents went to school to learn how to be a parent. They learned how to parent from watching their parents, who learned from watching theirs, and on and on. In most instances, but not exclusively, they teach not with love, affection, encouragement, and appreciation, but with yelling, punishment, violence, disrespect, and abuse. How many children do you think were *not* yelled at, scolded, hit, and/or punished? I suspect very few. And if they didn't get the negative messages in the home, they got it on the playground, in school, or someplace else.

In the face of such negativity, what do you think children decide about themselves? That they're brilliant, gorgeous, talented, and fabulous? Hardly. They usually decide that they must not be very smart, they're not good, something is wrong with them, they're not worthy, and they're not lovable. Under these circumstance, as a child matures into an adult, do you think he or she believes "I'm okay" or "I'm not okay"? I suspect your instinct is the same as mine. Not okay!

## My Story

Growing up, my life wasn't all that bad, but it wasn't all that great either. I grew up in an apartment in the Bronx, NY, with my mother, father, and older sister. On the surface, it was your typical American family. But here's what was happening below the surface:

My parents were the kind of people who, when I did what I was supposed to do, said nothing. I don't remember getting any particular acknowledgement or "atta-boys." On the other hand, when I didn't do what I was supposed to do, I heard plenty. The line "wait until your father gets home" was one I heard a lot.

Predictably, in the face of no acknowledgement for doing things well and lots of punishment for doing things wrong, I decided early on that I must not be very smart. And I also questioned whether I was a valuable human being who deserved to be loved (because I didn't feel like I was). I ultimately decided I wasn't a valuable human being. Those were decisions one and two.

My mother was someone who, again in my recollection, listened *what am I going to say next*. So around her, I had to work hard to get a word in edgewise. It didn't seem to me that my father wanted to work that hard, so slowly but surely he got quiet. I thought he was being a wimp (my interpretation), and someplace along the way I decided that I'd never let a woman dominate me the way she dominated him. That was decision number three.

My father was a hard working plumber. While we always had a place to live, clothes to wear, and food to eat, many times we couldn't do things I wanted to do because we couldn't afford it. Some of our relatives had a lot of money, but my father always spoke poorly of them. He blamed them for not helping him out. I made lots of decisions around that. I decided you had to work hard (decision number four), money was in short supply (number five), rich people aren't nice (number six), and we were not one of "them" (number seven). Does any of this sound familiar? Can you relate to any of these decisions?

I could go on and on, but I hope I've made my point. It's difficult, if not impossible in that paradigm, to emerge from childhood with your self-esteem intact, thinking you are okay. My conclusion, after looking at this for twenty some-odd years, is that we all have our version of "I'm not okay."

## This Process Impacts Us All

When I do retreats, I like to do a certain exercise with people to end the event. I've always thought the exercise would be a wonderful experience for people, but usually it's not. Here's the exercise: I tell people to close their eyes, and I ask them, "What's your gift? What makes you unique? What do you bring to life that's special?"

I then tell people to open their eyes and write down what came to mind as I asked those questions. Next, I ask people to come to the front of the room, one at a time, face their team members, and say, "My unique contribution to life is . . ." I guarantee you I have never had anyone stand up in front of a group and say, "I'm brilliant, gorgeous, talented, and fabulous."

Then I have all of their team members tell them what they left out. The person's job is to stand in front of the room and listen to what their fellow employees think of them. In *every* case, the people standing in front of the room are stunned to hear how well their teammates think of them and all of the wonderful attributes their co-workers think they have. Why? People's conversations about themselves are generally so negative and limiting that it's hard for them to hear all the acknowledgements. It's almost painful. In fact, it's not uncommon for people to try and dismiss what others say, for them to say "enough already," and for them to want the process to be over.

But I don't let it end quite yet. At this point, I ask everyone to get up and give the person in the front of the room a standing ovation, for about thirty seconds. Now, I don't know about you, but I love getting a standing ovation. It makes me feel like I did a good job. But for the typical person, it is painful to stand and be acknowledged that way. Almost every person tries to walk away after a few seconds. But I don't let them. They have to stand there and take it.

It sounds unbelievable, but it's true. Try it with your team. You'll see for yourself. People are so used to being criticized and criticizing themselves that to be acknowledged publicly is almost too much to take.

So that's why we have our attention on ourselves and why we are concerned with our survival. When you don't appreciate the truth of who you are; when you don't live in a conversation that you're brilliant, gorgeous, talented, and fabulous; when you actually think there is something wrong with you, you naturally have your attention on yourself. And, since it looks to you and me like everybody else is okay, and we're the only ones who have this issue, we feel adversarial with other people and naturally become concerned with our survival.

So, in our attempt to "make it" in this paradigm, we hop right on the "ladder of success" and start climbing toward the top. And, we've learned through the years that success means achieving "The American Dream" – you know, the house with the white picket fence, the Mercedes or BMW in the garage, the designer clothes, and more.

But here's the cruel joke. We think one day we'll get to the point on the ladder where we have accomplished enough that we will now feel okay. But this ignores the reality that the ladder is resting on a foundation of "not okay." Recall the conversation about satisfaction, which says that you can't get to anyplace other than where you start. In our paradigm, we start from "not okay." Unless we question that belief, every step of the way just reinforces that belief.

So you've accumulated all this "stuff," but you still feel "not okay." Instead of questioning the fundamental reason why you're climbing in the first place (because we don't consciously know the reason why), we conclude that we must need more "stuff." So we keep on climbing.

And we keep climbing and climbing, all the while being concerned with our survival, placing our attention on ourselves, wondering if we'll ever have enough, and feeling frustrated that we're not more peaceful and secure. We're convinced that everyone else has it made and that we are in competition with them. In the midst of all that thinking, we're supposed to be happy.

One of the things we used to do in the Lew Epstein clubs was have an annual meeting of all of the clubs. Every Memorial Day, men and women would gather at one of the club cities for this wonderful event. We had men's meetings, women's meetings, and joint meetings.

One year in the men's meeting, we had a couple of hundred men in a room, with Lew and Francine in the front leading the discussion. One man stood up and began to share what life was like for him. He was a company executive and had a lot of responsibilities. He shared that he spent much of his day scared about his responsibilities, that he often second guessed the decisions he made, that he was afraid to let people know about his insecurities because he didn't want them to view him as weak, and that he had many sleepless nights where all he could do was replay in his mind all that he had done during the day and question whether he did the "right" things.

I remember sitting in the room totally relating to what he was saying, for he might as well have been speaking for me. I started to feel a bit of relief, realizing there was a least one other person on the planet who had the same insecurities I had. I was amazed by his courage in getting up and sharing what he shared, being certain that the other men in the room likely were judging him and relating to him as weak.

Just then Lew, being the brilliant leader that he was, stopped the man, turned to the rest of us, and simply asked, "For how many of you men is this man speaking on your behalf?" *Every single hand went up!* Can you imagine? Every single hand went up. I was blown away. I couldn't believe it.

So the moment the speaker completed and sat down, my hand shot up. Lew called on me. I stood up, walked to the front of the room, looked at the assembly of men (all of whom *I* thought had their acts together), and asked, "Are you serious? Do every one of you really question whether you're good enough, smart enough, capable enough, like I do?" They all nodded their heads yes!

This was a life-changing event for me. At that moment I realized that I was not in this situation alone, that my conversation about me was not a unique conversation, that it was a conversation in the paradigm I had picked up along the way, and that we were all in this together. Now that didn't make my conversation about me go away, but at least I knew I wasn't alone and I didn't have to hide out any more. I didn't have to make believe I was okay when I didn't feel like I really was. It was very freeing.

## Your Conversation and You

Again it's time to pause. Are you clear yet that you live in a conversation? Think back to the exercise in Chapter 6 where I asked people to list the not-so-nice conversations they have about others and the wonderful things they could say about people. Which of the two do you think most accurately describes your conversation about you?

Are you critical of yourself? Do you second-guess yourself and beat yourself up for the "wrong" decisions or mistakes you make? Or do you relate to yourself as brilliant, gorgeous, talented, and fabulous?

Your answer here is important, because as long as you're critical of yourself, you'll be critical of others. That's just the way it is. To reach your full potential as a new paradigm leader, you have to commit to resolving the issues you have with you!

Here's the good news: to the degree you are critical of yourself, it's just a conversation.

Here's the bad news: to the degree you are critical of yourself, you listen to and think that conversation is the truth. And, you likely think you're the only one who has it.

But rest assured, you're not. We all have it. And part of becoming a conscious human being is to realize that and to move beyond it.

That Lew Epstein International Men's and Women's Club's annual retreat was a life-changing event for me. While I knew intellectually before that day that we all live in this "not okay" conversation, I hadn't let that sink in. And that day it really did. I finally got it that this is the conversation of the paradigm, and that it isn't personal to me. One of my coaches used to say that if you walk outside into a rainstorm, you would get wet, yet you wouldn't think it was a personal rainstorm.

In fact, the rainstorm is a great metaphor. We are all living in this rainstorm and getting wet, yet we take it personally. It's time to stop doing that. It's time to take a stand for your worth and value. It's time to stop listening to that voice that tells you you're not good enough, smart enough, talented enough, capable enough, and whatever other "not enough's" there are. As I've said, it's just a conversation that you picked up when you were two or three or four or whenever. But it's not the truth about *who you are.*

There is a wonderful passage in *A Return to Love* by Marianne Williamson. It goes like this:

> Our deepest fear is not that we are inadequate.
> Our deepest fear is that we are powerful beyond measure.
> It is our light, not our darkness, that most frightens us.
> We ask ourselves, who am I to be brilliant,
> gorgeous, talented and fabulous?
> Actually, who are you *not* to be?
> You are a child of God.
> Your playing small doesn't serve the world.
> There's nothing enlightened about shrinking so that
> other people won't feel insecure around you.
> We were born to make manifest the glory of
> God that is within us.
> It's not just in some of us; it's in everyone.
> And as we let our own light shine, we unconsciously
> give other people permission to do the same.
> As we are liberated from our own fears,
> our presence automatically liberates others.

Another equally moving sentiment comes from an Arthur Miller play. It goes like this:

> I dreamed I had a child, and even in the dream I saw it was my life, and it was an idiot, and I ran away. But it always crept into my lap again, clutched at my clothes. Until I thought, if I could kiss it, whatever in it was my own, perhaps I could sleep. And I bent to its broken face, and it was horrible... but I kissed it. I think one must finally take one's life in one's arms.

Take your life in your arms! Give up whatever conversation has you be "not enough." Take a stand for your greatness. You are brilliant, gorgeous, talented, and fabulous. That's the truth. You were born to make manifest the glory of however you relate to the source of all life that has you be. And, as you let your own light shine and stop being critical of yourself, you begin to see the magnificence in others. You begin to create a space in your organization for everyone else to experience his or her own magnificence. It's truly a win/win game.

If this mindset change is a struggle for you, get a coach. There are many coaches today who work with people on this issue, and I'm sure you can find one on the Internet. Go to the web site of the International Coach Federation, www.coachfederation.org, and use its referral service to find the perfect coach for you.

*To laugh often and much, to win the respect of intelligent people and the respect of children; to earn the appreciation of honest critics and endure the betrayal of false friends; to appreciate beauty, to find the best in others, to give of oneself; to leave the world a bit better, whether by a healthy child, a garden patch or a redeemed social condition, to have played and laughed with enthusiasm and sung with exultation; to know even one life has breathed easier; this is to have succeeded.*

✦ Ralph Waldo Emerson

## Chapter 12

# Complaints and Gossip

TO SURVIVE in the existing paradigm, we develop various techniques. Two of the most common are 1) to complain and 2) to gossip. As used herein, a complaint is an expression of discontent with a person or a situation, and gossip is making a derogatory statement to someone about a third person. Do you notice how often the people around you complain? Do you notice the ongoing complaints that *you* have? Before you continue, write down one or two of your favorite complaints to test the following discussion.

When I first start working in a company, one of the most debilitating realities I often encounter is the amount and severity of the gossip. Many reasons exist for this, one of which we'll discuss here in conjunction with complaints. We'll discuss the other in Chapter 13.

In his treatise *The Passions, The Myth and Nature of Human Emotion* (University of Notre Dame Press, 1983) Robert C. Solomon says, "Every emotion is a strategy, a purposive attempt to structure our world in such a way as to maximize our sense of personal dignity and self-esteem. And, as strategies, our emotions can be more or less successful, more or less direct, well or ill conceived, effective or self-defeating . . . Every passion endows our lives with meaning, but every meaning is not ultimately meaningful, ultimately successful in maximizing our dignity and self-esteem and making possible the mutual respect and intimacy we desire."

In other words, Solomon says that everything a human being does when his self-esteem is in question and he's concerned with his survival is a strategy. These strategies can be either well or ill conceived. Survival strategies fall in the latter category.

Why do we do them? As Solomon says, "to maximize our sense of personal dignity and self-esteem." We want to feel okay in order to counter the underlying feeling of not okay. But strategies, while they do have this payoff, also have a big cost.

So people go around complaining and gossiping. Co-workers complain and gossip about each other, their supervisors, the company, everything. Management complains about the employees, the economy, the competition, the salespeople. It's a very popular game. Don't take responsibility; don't do anything about your complaint; don't take action; just settle for complaining and gossiping.

Here's another way of looking at what people get when they complain or gossip. First, they get to make somebody or something wrong, which, of course, makes them "right." They get to justify who they are and what they are doing, and they get to invalidate who the other person is and what he or she is doing. All of this makes them look good, again maximizing their sense of personal dignity and self-esteem.

## The Vicious Cycle

The alternative to complaining is to confront the issue and take action. And, indeed, some people do this some of the time. When they don't, the payoff is that they get to blame the other, avoid any responsibility in the matter, play safe, and avoid risk by not confronting the other person.

So that's what we often do. We'll talk about the antidote later; but for now, recognize that a big survival game is likely going on in your company. Rather than taking responsibility, risking, and getting into action, people settle for looking good, being right, justifying themselves, and blaming others, all so they can feel good about themselves.

As stated previously, we pay a big price for this game. Remember the list of consequences for listening unconsciously, with your attention on yourself and being concerned with your survival? The same list applies here. There is no communication, no understanding, no appreciation of the other person's position, no intimacy, and certainly no trust. That costs you satisfaction, happiness, a sense of well being, self-confidence, joy, aliveness, and ultimately the relationship. In a business setting, it costs productivity, creativity, teamwork, enthusiasm, turnover, success, and of course, money, results, and accomplishment.

But there's more. When you complain and/or gossip instead of taking action, you turn yourself into a victim. After all, it's not *your* fault. "I can't do anything about it," you say, and that's the real definition of a victim. So you have two choices: 1) take responsibility or 2) be a victim. Many people choose the latter. I don't recommend it, and choice two certainly isn't the choice a leader in the new paradigm we are creating would make.

When you go around complaining and/or gossiping, you have no possibility of genuine satisfaction. Yes, there is the brief satisfaction that comes from being right and making the other person wrong, but that's not genuine satisfaction.

When I do executive retreats, I take time for each participant to "tell one on himself" – to admit what he is complaining and/or gossiping about and what he is getting out of it. I then have people assess what it costs them to do that. I do this because people will only give up these survival games when they know what it's costing them. Otherwise, they have no reason to stop playing. People love to be right and look good . . . that is until they see what they give up for being right and looking good.

This is a time for people to get authentic. Complaints are an inauthentic way of being because complaining makes you look like you want something to happen, something to be different, but you really don't. If you really did want something different, you'd take action. What you really want are the payoffs! It's all about survival, about being right, about making other people wrong, about looking good, etc., all to maximize your sense of personal dignity and self-esteem.

In every company where I've encountered it, gossip is a killer. It sucks the life out of everyone. People have the ability to be productive and creative, but not in the presence of gossip. When there's gossip, people's focus is on what's wrong and what's not working rather than on what's possible. Welcome to life in the 21$^{st}$ century!

Here's what's really sad. The results a company experiences are a direct function of who people are being, what their collective energy is focused on, the aliveness they bring to work, and their degree of alignment. Think back to our discussion of cause and effect and my definition of a successful organization: a group of enthusiastic, confident, positive people working together on behalf of a future they have all committed themselves to. How can such a group prevail in an environment of gossip?

Every company has a mood. It's not something we pay a lot of attention to, but it's what we should pay more attention to than anything else. Yes, there is an economy out there. Yes, there is competition. But neither the economy nor the competition will ever do you in. Only you can do you in. If people focus their energy on making each other wrong, being right, being frustrated, being skeptical, and being resigned rather than working together on behalf of an exciting future they have all committed themselves to, then it's going to be a long and tough road ahead.

So where do we go from here? What's your job as a leader committed to the success of your enterprise? How do you make work work? It all depends on where you start. You have to *start* from being a happy group of satisfied, enthusiastic, optimistic, joyous, alive people with faith and trust in you and the future, working together on behalf of a future you are all committed to. That, more than anything else, is your job. Get that accomplished and the rest will take care of itself.

*The reasonable man adapts himself to the conditions that
surround him . . .*

*The unreasonable man adapts the surrounding
conditions to himself . . .*

*All progress depends on the unreasonable man.*

⅃ George Bernard Shaw

*Chapter 13*

# The Dynamics of Our Relationships

BEFORE WE turn our attention to how to bring this all together, it's necessary to discuss how everything we've discussed plays out in our working relationships. In the beginning of this discussion I said that we live in a particular paradigm. It isn't good and it isn't bad. It just is what it is. It has us be and act in a particular way. So *it*, not you or I, is responsible for our world being the way it is. The existing paradigm, the one right here and right now, is *not* set up to have a group of enthusiastic, confident, positive people working together on behalf of a future they have all committed themselves to. To the contrary, it is set up to have pettiness, gossiping, competition, conflict, arguments, and righteousness.

We live in a world where people think they are not okay. They have their attention on themselves, are concerned with their survival, are trying to make it, and are coming from fear and scarcity. It's not exactly a formula for success. But that's the condition under which people wake up and go to work. And, as you can imagine, it produces the result it is designed for: pettiness, gossiping, competition, conflict, arguments, and righteousness.

So let's explore how this impacts our relationships. Then we'll talk about how to clean up the mess that we make. Finally, we'll design a new paradigm for the 21$^{st}$ century and beyond. While the discussion about relationships will primarily focus on business relationships, everything said here applies to our personal relationships as well. So please read on with the broadest possible listening.

## The First Encounter

All relationships start the same way. Someone comes to work in your company. You meet her and she meets you. The people already there meet her and vice versa. Often, not always, the people experience an initial honeymoon stage. Everyone seems to be happy, and it looks like things will work. But what do we know about all honeymoons? They are usually all too brief and eventually end!

This is predictable and inevitable, because human beings have expectations. We are expectation-generating machines. We produce expectations so fast that if you could actually see it happening, it would make your head spin. It's part of the not okay survival mechanism.

We have expectations about what the person will be like, what the relationship will be like, how the person will perform, how hard he'll work, what his capabilities and talents are, and on and on. And, especially in a business context, human beings have intentions. We intend something to happen, some result to be produced, and some end product to be accomplished. We don't hire someone to do nothing. We intend for him to produce results.

It's not unusual in business for employers, employees, and co-workers to discuss some of these expectations and intentions. More often than not, we never state the true expectations and intentions, and we generate new ones on a daily basis. The fact that this happens isn't bad or wrong; it just happens. And it's entirely human.

## The Let Down

Have you ever met anyone who fulfilled your expectations and lived up to your intentions all the time? While it would be wonderful if you could honestly say yes, the answer is likely no. So the only predictable result is that your expectations will be unfulfilled and your intentions will be thwarted. Whenever this occurs, you end up disappointed.

Again, this is natural and to be expected. Since it's virtually impossible to stop having expectations, being disappointed is a part of life.

But here's where we get ourselves in trouble. During workshops and speeches, I ask the attendees: "When you notice that you're disappointed, how many of you can honestly say that you *always* go over to the other person and communicate your disappointment to him or her?" A few hands may go up, but usually over 95% of the people admit they don't do that. At the very least, they admit that they don't do it all of the time.

Again, we have a number of valid reasons for this, and they all center around fear. Given that we are always concerned with our survival, communicating something distasteful threatens our survival. And if the disappointment is with a supervisor, manager, or executive, we fear that communicating threatens our job, our income, or our relationship with that person.

Of course, since nobody ever really taught us *how* to communicate, we simply don't know how to speak without judgment. Our past experiences in communicating disappointments are usually negative, so we certainly don't want to rock the boat. We assume our communication will trigger an upset. People often tell me they don't want to hurt the other person's feelings. However, my belief is that the person doesn't want to deal with the upset that will certainly occur.

Perhaps the biggest reason people don't communicate, as I've discussed in Chapter 9, is that people do not know how to listen. You can almost count on people to get defensive and to take your communication personally. Maybe they'll wait patiently until you are finished, maybe not. Either way, we expect them to launch into a defense and counter attack. So it seems better to not say anything and stuff it. But is it?

Instead of communicating, we go into the metaphorical file room in our mind, find an empty file folder, put the other person's name on the folder, and deposit the undelivered communication (the disappointment, the unfulfilled expectation, the thwarted intention) into the file. We then file it away for the time being. Then the next disappointment occurs, or the same one repeats itself, and we make another entry into the file . . . and then another, and another.

## The Result

During the honeymoon period everything is so wonderful because you're not dealing with a lot of disappointments. You can be open and intimate with the other person, and you usually have a high degree of trust. So on the scale of openness, intimacy, and trust, you could say that 100% is available to you.

But every entry you put in the "file" displaces the possibility of 100% openness, intimacy, and trust. Think of it like a glass of water that's filled to the brim. The water represents openness, intimacy, and trust. If you start pouring sand into the glass, where the sand represents the undelivered communications, then it's evident that the water will soon start spilling out.

So one day you have 100% openness, intimacy, and trust, and you feel wonderful about the other person. But before you know it, you're down to 90%. Ninety percent isn't all that bad, but it doesn't feel quite as good as 100%. You're not quite as eager to be open with the other person, but it's not too bad.

However, the sand keeps going into the glass, the disappointments keep going into the file, and now you're down to 80% on the scale of openness, intimacy, and trust. You're starting to suffer a bit. It's getting harder and harder to be with the other person and to talk openly and honestly. You start avoiding, maybe being a bit sarcastic, but you continue on.

You can see where this is going. Eventually you get to the point where you will not put up with it any further. This is when your mind starts to play a very interesting game with you. When this process of making entries into the file first started, at some level you knew you contributed something to this upset, and you knew you should have communicated your feelings to the other person. But you didn't and you still don't because of all the reasons we've discussed. As the "file" gets bigger and bigger you lose all sense of your responsibility, and you become convinced that the source of your increasing upset really is the other person. "If he would just . . . (fill in the blank)."

## The Mood Shifts

At this point, one of several things happens. In personal relationships, people fight and argue and perhaps split up or get divorced. I'm convinced that these withheld communications are the primary reason why most personal relationships turn sour or end. In business, people start to complain and gossip or they simply leave. Or, have you ever been in a situation where you said or did something, and another person reacted in a way that was dramatically disproportionate to what you said or did? Of course! Have you ever been in a situation where somebody else said or did something, and you reacted in a way that was dramatically disproportionate to what the other person said or did? Of course you did that too.

I call that "file emptying time." You (or the other person) don't react just to what was said or done at that moment; you react with all the fury that exists in the accumulated file. Given that the reaction is totally out of proportion to what just happened, the recipient of the file dumping is caught off guard and is bewildered, almost guaranteeing that he or she will take the communication personally, get defensive, and attack back. It's an ugly situation, and one we have all had an opportunity to experience.

Sometimes, instead of the file emptying, the other person becomes the enemy. You drift apart and fight about everything. The file becomes evidence of something negative about the other person, and you start to use the file against him and make him wrong. It's another version of the survival game. And, of course, the payoff is that you get to be right.

I've gone into organizations and experienced these occurrences in many forms. Sometimes people learn to be polite with each other, but you can feel the underlying tension. Everybody knows it's there, but nobody is willing to confront it. So people become like strangers in the night, exchanging pleasantries and doing the best they can to make the most of a bad situation and get on with what they have to do. Definitely not a formula for a championship team.

Sometimes it's worse. I've gone into organizations where it seems that people come to work, climb into their foxholes, arm themselves, and dare anyone to walk into their space. It can get ugly.

## How it All Unfolds

In 2001, I gave a speech to a group of people in the office building and management business. After the speech, the president of a real estate development company that had four operating divisions – development, construction, property management, and leasing – came to talk to me. There was also a finance department, and each had one or more executives heading it up. In total, there were nine people, including the president, human resources manager, and information services manager on the management team.

During the conversation that ensued, I asked the president how the relationships were between the executives. His answer was that they were awful (he used a different word, but I want to keep it clean). So I went to the company's headquarters and interviewed all nine of them. As always, I found lots of judgments, withheld communications, and disappointments. The woman who headed up development was very aggressive, which is probably what you want in someone in that position. But she did a lot of things that people didn't understand. She never bothered to explain her reasons, and they never bothered to ask. As a result, nobody trusted her.

The people in construction were convinced that the people in finance did everything they could possibly do to make their lives miserable and, of course, the people in finance couldn't understand why the people in construction were so difficult to deal with. The gentleman in leasing had insecurities about how the president felt regarding his performance, was somewhat convinced he was disappointing the president, but never bothered to verify any of his assumptions. The president didn't have a clue how to handle any of this, and he hoped it would somehow handle itself. Surprisingly, the company was pretty darn good and successful.

What happened here, and what happens all the time, is that people generate a conversation – a listening about the other people – and that becomes who they are for them. It's no longer a judgment or opinion; they *are* that way. Our listening becomes the space in which they get to show up. And they just keep showing up that way, and we get to be right once again.

### The Reality of Life Revealed

We've gone as deeply into the existing paradigm as is necessary to understand why most, if not nearly all organizations, don't fit my definition of a successful organization; that is, a group of enthusiastic, confident, positive people working together on behalf of a future they have all committed themselves to.

When you grow up in a world where you learn to believe that you are not okay, where you have your attention on yourself, where you are concerned with your own survival, when you come from fear and scarcity, when you look for satisfaction and happiness in the circumstances of life, when you listen right/wrong, get to the point, etc., when you use language to talk about what you think is there rather than using it to create what's there, when you withhold your communications and complain, gossip, and build files, you certainly don't have a formula for success, happiness, and joy. But that's the world we inherited, and that's the reality. It doesn't pay to fight it. It makes a lot more sense to understand it, acknowledge it, and get to work putting in the antidote. That is what the remaining chapters will discuss.

*I have caught life. I have come down with life. I was a wisp of undifferentiated nothingness, and then a little peephole opened quite suddenly. Light and sound poured in. Voices began to describe me and my surroundings. Nothing they said could be appealed. The said I was a boy named Rudolph Waltz, and that was that. They said the year was 1932, and that was that. They said I was in Midland City, Ohio, and that was that.*

*They never shut up. Year after year they piled detail upon detail. They do it still. You know what they say now? They say the year is 1982, and that I am fifty years old.*

*Blah blah blah*

❧ Kurt Vonnegut

*Chapter 14*

# Cleaning up the Mess

BEFORE WE move forward to design a new paradigm, you may need to first "clean up the mess" that you or others in your company have made as a result of being with each other in the way discussed in Chapter 13. In just about every company I've worked with, unspoken upsets and disappointments are there, so we are not dealing with a clean slate. To create a mutually satisfying future on top of the unspoken upsets would be like trying to build a skyscraper on swampland. The unresolved upsets will weaken the foundation of the new paradigm, making a meaningful and satisfying result impossible.

The number one requirement for cleaning up the messes people make in their relationships is that they have to be willing. They must be willing to go back in time and clean out the trash. They must be willing to let go of it – not to get even or dump – but to let go.

In my experience, people need to be not only willing, but also anxious to clean up the mess they've made in their relationships with each other to restore the intimacy, openness, and trust and to get their relationships back.

Usually, people are willing and anxious, but occasionally there are a few who have such a vested interest in being right and in winning that even the offer of peace and harmony is not appealing. You might run into people like this yourself.

## Moving Ahead

I remember the first time I did a retreat. It was for a group of partners of a law firm in Texas. Two firms with very different cultures had merged, and the clashes were predictable and regular. They had hired three different consultants over a three-year period, but each failed to bridge the gap between the two groups. The firm's administrator called to see if I could help.

I did the retreat with one of my associates at the time, a gentleman named Craig. We took the fifteen partners to the same hotel they had been to four years in a row. We met in one of the hotel's meeting rooms and began by talking with them, asking questions and getting feedback. After several hours, we said to them: "We are now going to take a break. For the last few hours we've been courting you, inviting you into a game that will heal your relationships with each other and leave you in action, working together on behalf of a future you can all be committed to. It's now time to get the work done. If, after everything we've said, you don't feel like you want to participate, you should honor your integrity, tell us you are not willing to participate, and leave."

As soon as we started the break, one of the partners came over to us and said he was leaving. When we asked him why, he said that it all sounded like a bunch of BS to him, that most of his partners were assholes, and that he didn't think this would do any good. So he left. He is an example of someone who was so committed to being right that he was not willing to give the process a try. He couldn't see the forest for the trees.

The good news is that people like him are few and far between. Most people are cautious, but they're willing to move ahead. Now it's time to learn what moving ahead looks like.

## Towards a Partnership Paradigm

The intention is for you to use the information presented thus far so you and others in your company will know how to talk to each other, how to speak and listen, and how to responsibly communicate unfulfilled expectations, thwarted intentions, and disappointments so you and they can empty the files and return to where your relationships started, a place of openness, intimacy, and trust. Under those circumstances, you can begin to design a new paradigm for being that will allow for true teamwork and what I call "partnership."

The "file emptying" is a five-step process.

## Step One: Take an Inventory

The first step is to write down what's in the file. Here are the statements I recommend you use:

> My expectations of you that are unfulfilled are . . .
> My intentions for you/us that have been thwarted are . . .
> I am disappointed with you/our relationship in that . . .
> What I'm not saying to you is . . .
> What I am not acknowledging you for is . . .

Before I tell you what this accomplishes, try it for yourself. Pick someone in your company who you have things to say to – unfulfilled expectations, thwarted intentions, and disappointments – and take some time to write down your answers to the above statements. You will find the exercise quite revealing.

❧

This step serves several purposes. First, you are writing about yourself. Remember, when you're upset with someone, your mind convinces you that the source of the upset is the other person. These statements force you to look at the upset from the perspective of responsibility, which is a fundamental intention of this whole exercise. Once people begin to see that the real source of their upset is *their* unfulfilled expectations and *their* thwarted intentions, the desire to blame the other person begins to dissipate.

Second, when a person is upset, the upset seems like this huge mass of things that are wrong with the other person. Realize that the mind is not a very useful place to store and sort out upsets. By getting your thoughts down on paper, you begin to notice there wasn't as much to the "file" as you thought, and you see that your upsets and disappointments stem from a few, manageable issues.

Third, people consistently report they already start feeling better once they get their feelings on paper. Getting the disappointments out of their head begins to dissipate the energy that the upset contains.

## Step Two : Communicate

### How to Speak

If you were going to communicate everything in your "file" to another person, how would you manage your communication? It's evident that being accusatory, yelling, finger pointing, and attacking would be non-productive. Instead, speak to the other person with respect and compassion. After all, there is another human being on the other side of your communication.

Remain calm, be open and honest, and say exactly what you need to say without sugar coating it. Listeners find it annoying if they feel the speaker is trying to protect their feelings by being "nice."

At the same time, it's critical that you not be righteous, but rather communicate from a place of responsibility. If you become righteous, the listener will feel like you are "wronging" him, and he will want to justify and defend himself, all of which will defeat the purpose of the exercise.

At this point many people ask, "Why would I want to say it all, especially the things I don't want to confront?" I hope the answer is obvious. You need to completely empty the file, for it's only when the file is completely empty that there can be 100% openness, intimacy, and trust. If you leave anything in the file, it becomes like a cancer that can only grow and eventually cause another upset.

Some of the things we learned as children keep us stuck in the existing paradigm. One of these childhood messages is that if you don't have something good to say, you shouldn't say anything. If we took this instruction literally, we would never communicate our upsets and disappointments, and our inevitable files would just grow and grow. Obviously, that old childhood message is not very useful.

### How to Listen

If someone were going to tell you everything in her file, how would you listen? From our discussion thus far, you certainly know how *not* to listen. The way to listen is to "*just get it!*" Listen with compassion. Get your attention off yourself, get over there with the other person, and get how it is for her. Re-create what it must be like for the speaker.

Encourage the other person to say everything, and say nothing in response other than "thank you" or "I'm sorry" or both. Do not react, do not listen as if you're being made wrong, and don't take anything the other person says personally, even though it is personal.

You might think this is a set-up for something really painful. After all, you're going to sit there and listen while somebody says all kinds of things about you, and all you get to do is thank them, perhaps say you're sorry, and encourage them to say more.

Rest assured that there is a good reason for being willing to listen in this way. First, people have the experience of being heard, which is enormously satisfying and fulfilling. Second, it allows the speaker to empty his file. And what's in it for you is the rehabilitation of the relationship, which is something both parties truly want.

Equally important, you'll learn things about yourself, the other person, and what's going on in your company that will surely amaze or surprise you.

I did this work with a client company in Florida. When I told the COO that I would give his managers an opportunity to communicate everything in their files to him and his job was to "just get it" and say thank you, he thought it would be difficult. Reluctantly he agreed to try it.

When I spoke to him after the event, his reaction was typical. He said that while he heard some things he expected, he was truly amazed at some of the feedback people gave him. He had no idea that some of the things that had happened at the company had impacted his managers the ways they did. Some people said things that were completely opposite of what he thought. While I guarantee you it wasn't easy for him to listen to some of the things said, he was profoundly appreciative of going through the experience.

When I do this in a retreat environment, I have each person take a turn sitting in a chair in the middle of the room. Everyone then tells the person what they have been "filing." The speaker uses the five statements from step one as a guide, and the listener gets to listen. He doesn't respond; he just gets the other persons' communication.

Now you may be asking, "Isn't this embarrassing, a horrible experience, to ask someone to sit in front of all of his peers and have them communicate their unfulfilled expectations, their thwarted intentions, their disappointments? Wouldn't it be better to do this one-on-one and privately?" Actually no, and for several reasons.

First, if you want to build a sense of team, you need to end the "private" communications. Everybody knows what's going on anyway, so it's time to stop pretending to keep this all a "secret."

Second, if John were to communicate to Fred privately, it would be very easy for Fred to ignore what John says and deflect the value in the communication, thinking it's only John's issue. But if Fred is sitting in a room with all his team members, and several people (or everyone) communicate the same thing to him, it's pretty darn hard to ignore the comments.

There are always things that people do that are upsets to others, and most of the time we don't know what they are or what the impact is because nobody tells us. But when you're sitting in a room, surrounded by your team members, with all of them communicating their unfulfilled expectations, thwarted intentions, and disappointments, it's impossible to not have the feedback sink in.

With the fifteen Texas law firm partners I discussed earlier, it took half of the first day and most of the second day to complete step two. Each partner had the opportunity to communicate all the disappointments that had developed over the years since the merger, all of the unfulfilled expectations about how they would work together, and all of the thwarted intentions in the results that didn't get produced.

As I sat in the room and watched this process, I felt the hurtful energy in the room dissipate as the upsets were communicated and released. And, in the process, people were learning to take responsibility for their upsets and disappointments, to communicate responsibly, and to listen with compassion.

When we started day three of this particular retreat, we went around the room and asked if anybody had anything to share before we continued. One of the partners responded that his wife had called him earlier that morning to ask how it was going. He related that he told his wife he had witnessed a miracle, and if he hadn't witnessed what he had seen with his own eyes, he wouldn't have believed it. Everyone else in the room said they felt the same way. So rather than being a horrible experience, it was totally liberating. That continued to be the identical reaction from the hundreds of people who have gone through the same process.

In another firm we worked with, over forty people attended the retreat. Given the impracticality of having everyone communicate to each person individually, we had each participant come up to the front of the room and say whatever he or she wasn't saying to the group in general and/or to someone in particular.

The first day of this retreat was fairly uneventful, with no major revelations or disappointments. The morning of the second day, however, one of the participants got up in front of the group and, in great detail and with a great amount of emotion, spoke about his ten years as a practicing alcoholic, all of which time he was a member of this firm. Now, he hadn't had a drink for eight years and regularly went to AA meetings, but it was a big secret he lived with. In AA, one of the twelve steps is to make amends, but he didn't know how to do that with such a large group of partners. This became his opportunity.

I stood at the side of the room and listened with compassion, which was the instruction given to everyone else. As he emptied his file, I was so moved by his open and honest sharing that tears started to stream down my face. I reached for my handkerchief. That's when I noticed that virtually everyone in the room was also reaching for a tissue (we always have boxes of tissues at these events). By the time he finished, there wasn't a dry eye in the house. And upon his completion, everyone leaped to their feet and gave him a standing ovation. It was an extraordinary experience none of us who were there will ever forget. But more important, the process of bonding and building a sense of team among this group had begun

As soon as he sat down, a hand in the back of the room shot up. So I asked, "Oh, are you next?" He said, "Absolutely. If I don't do this now, I'll never do it." So this next partner comes up to the front of the room, turns to his partners and says, "What I'm not saying to you is that I'm gay." He then proceeded to say more about his sexual preference and his gay relationships.

When he was done, one of the other partners stood up and asked, "Are you crazy? We know you're gay; we've always known you're gay. You're not our gay partner John; you're our partner John."

John stood there in disbelief. He had been with this firm for twenty-eight years, and all that time he lived with this secret. But the only one who thought it was a secret was him! At the end of the day, when we went around the room and gave everyone a chance to say what they wanted to say to be complete for the day, John stood up and said, "This is the happiest day of my whole life!"

That's what our current paradigm is costing people – not having the freedom to communicate, not having any real listening, not having the opportunity to be heard. I'd venture to say that's what's likely going on with the people in your company and in your life, with your co-workers, your employees, your family, and your friends. It's not because you're bad or wrong; rather, it's because you're a human being. And now you can change all of that.

## Step Three: Apologize

Step three is to apologize. Unfortunately, most people do not understand and appreciate the power of an apology.

People frequently think that the phrase "I apologize" means "I'm sorry." It doesn't. And while people in our culture often use the two terms interchangeably, I'm a purist and think you shouldn't do that. The word "sorry" is derived from the word "sorrow." So, in essence, when you say, "I'm sorry," you're saying "I feel sad" or "I experience sorrow over that." "I'm sorry" is an expression of your feelings. That is why, when people are sitting in the center and others are communicating to them, we let them say "I'm sorry" if someone says something that generates sadness in them.

"I apologize," on the other hand, means something entirely different. "I apologize" includes three distinct elements. First, it's an acknowledgement. I acknowledge what you said; I acknowledge what I did or didn't do; I acknowledge what I said or didn't say; I acknowledge the substance of your communication.

Second, it's a willingness to take responsibility. Third, it's a request for forgiveness.

### *How This Works*

After the Texas law firm retreat, the partners decided to let all their employees empty their files to the partners. Because there were many employees, we divided them into groups of thirty and spent the morning training them in this speaking and listening approach. After lunch, we had the partners come and sit in the front of the room, and each employee had an opportunity to say what he or she was not saying.

One secretary turned to one of the partners and said: "Paul, what I'm not saying to you is that when I pass you in the hall in the morning, I say 'good morning'. But you don't respond. So when you are gone, I turn to the wall and say 'good morning' to the wall. I want you to know I get more satisfaction saying 'good morning' to the wall than I get in saying 'good morning' to you, because I don't expect a response from the wall!"

Her words were an embarrassment and a blow to Paul. But Paul wasn't a bad guy. Actually, he was a good guy. Like many of us, though, he was unconscious and so focused on himself that he was often oblivious to what was going on around him. Her words were a huge wake up call. Because he was so unaware of this, he was profoundly appreciative of this secretary saying what she said.

All Paul could do was apologize. He couldn't go back and change what had happened. He could only clean up the consequences and hurt feelings about what happened and move forward from there.

He apologized by saying, "I apologize for not paying attention to you, for not being appreciative of your desire to be friendly, for not responding to you, and for appearing like an insensitive, uncaring, unappreciative jerk." (The last word wasn't necessary, but it helped her have the experience of being heard.) He acknowledged what she said, acknowledged what he did or didn't do, took responsibility, and while not stated, he invited her to forgive him. She did.

People are often reluctant to apologize because they feel an apology is an admission of wrong or guilt. They think that by apologizing, they are saying, "I was bad. I was wrong. You were right." Since human beings always want to be right and look good, that is a significant barrier to apologizing.

One of the most valuable lessons you can learn from this book is that the above perception is not what an apology means. Not at all. An apology is truly a gift that you give to the other person. It doesn't make you look weak at all. Just the opposite. It allows others to have that wonderful experience of being heard, which they much appreciate. Rather than appearing weak, you show up as their hero.

My friend and mentor Lew Epstein was fond of saying that when you were born, you were given an infinite supply of apologies. So make sure you use them up before you die.

I once worked with seven partners of a firm who had grown up with each other. They all met when they were teenagers and came to live in a drug rehabilitation facility. As they freed themselves from their addictions, they worked together in the facility. When their work at the facility came to an end, they decided to take their experience and enter the business world as partners in a commercial enterprise.

As you can imagine, because they had been together for so long, they had quite a few things stuffed in their files. In our first retreat, they cleared the air and revealed all that they had been holding in. The amazing part was when we came to the apologies. They apologized to each other for over two hours. They were so committed to making sure everyone had the experience of being heard that they were unwilling to leave out anything. They apologized sincerely for all the things they could each see they did that was in any way hurtful to any of the others. They finally empted their files.

## Step Four: Forgiveness

Step four of the file emptying process is forgiveness. The definition I use of forgiveness is:

> To give up resentment against or the desire to punish; stop being angry with; pardon. To give up the claim to punish or exact penalty for (an offense); overlook. To give as before.

The last sentence captures what forgiveness is really all about. The actual word "forgiveness" comes from the expression "to give as before." It means that you return yourself to the place you were at before the transgression you are forgiving someone for. You wipe the slate clean, start all over, and let go.

Because of the influence of the existing paradigm, most people are not very good at forgiving. We want to be right; we don't want to take responsibility; we like to blame, look good, justify ourselves, and invalidate others. For those and many other reasons, when somebody does something that offends us, we automatically assume he is at fault and we are justified in our anger and upset. But that's not a formula for peace or happiness. Not forgiving is like picking up a handful of hot coals to throw at another person, or taking poison and waiting for the other person to die.

In other words, when we don't forgive, we are the ones who suffer. We think we are happy because we are right, but we aren't happy. We are the ones carrying around the anger and hurt. The majority of the time the other person doesn't even have a clue that we are angry and upset, so she certainly doesn't suffer.

And there's more. A major article in the October 23, 2003 issue of *USA Today* has the headline: "Forgiveness could be balm for the body, too." Some of the things the article says are:

> Overall, findings show a link between forgiveness and health, says Everett Worthington, executive director of the group (A Campaign for Forgiveness Research, a non-profit organization that promotes studies). "Chronic unforgiveness causes stress," he says. "Every time people think of their transgressor, their body responds."
>
> Blood pressure and heart rates go up. Facial muscles tense, stress hormones kick in. Chronic stress affects the immune and cardiovascular systems, he says. Forgiveness reduces stress by replacing "negative emotions with positive ones."

During retreats, or whenever I facilitate a file emptying between individuals or groups of individuals, I ask the individuals if they are willing to forgive each other. I make it clear that there are three choices. "Yes," "No," and "I'm committed to it, but not prepared to do it yet; I'll work on it and keep you posted."

I always put in the third alternative so people can choose authentically. Sometimes it's not so simple to forgive. In my own life, one of my daughters carried a lot of hurt from her childhood about who I was for her during those early years. We sat many times and talked about it. She would empty her file and cry, and I would apologize, but her hurt wouldn't go away. She would periodically leave, heal, get some help, and come back and try to forgive again. It took her many years to get to the bottom of it and finally forgive, but the good news is that she finally did.

Friends of mine, a married couple, had a similar ordeal. At one point in the marriage, the wife chose to have an affair with another man. She quickly learned that an affair was not what she wanted. The affair actually strengthened her commitment to the marriage, so she ended the affair. But she was clear she could not live with the consequences of keeping the affair a secret from her husband. She felt that the risk of telling him was clearly less than the risk of keeping it a secret.

So she told him. The details of what happened are not that relevant. He said what he said; she said what she said. She apologized and expressed her commitment to the relationship. But forgiving her was not something he could easily do. She said that the next year was like living in hell. But he was committed to forgiving her, and over time he did.

Similar situations exist in business. Fortunately, in over 98% of the cases, people are smart enough to realize that if they don't forgive, the only ones they hurt are themselves, and so they forgive. There are occasional occurrences where people opt for choice three: they are committed to forgiving and say that they will work on it. And there are rare occurrences where people won't forgive, which, by the way, isn't so bad. If you discover there is someone in your organization who would rather be right than forgive, that is very useful information, as they just might not be the kind of person you want in your company.

Remember the lawyer who left the retreat in Texas? At the end of the retreat, the partners who stayed were so thrilled with the result that they decided to do the retreat again and include some people who couldn't make the first one. When they invited the lawyer who left to participate, he refused. So they invited him to leave the firm, which he did. The ones who remained were much better off because they didn't have to deal with his ever-present anger.

## Step Five: Completion

Now we're ready to complete the process, and that's what step five is for. If I were a minister and what I just described to you were a wedding ceremony, I would pronounce you man and wife and say you can now kiss the bride. But I am not a minister, and this is not a wedding ceremony; it is another kind of ceremony. So while I don't know what you will feel is appropriate to do, I do know that at the appropriate time you'll look into your heart and know what you need to do.

In my experience, people always know what to do. Depending on the level of intimacy that exists in the group, several things happen. Men, especially those who have a hard time being intimate, shake hands and sometimes exchange a brief hug. For other people, the hugs are more meaningful. I've seen many people hug each other for extended periods. I've also seen a fair amount of tears shed as people express their appreciation for what they have just been through and their sadness and regret for not doing it sooner. In any event, the files are emptied, the air is clean and fresh, and people are ready for a new beginning.

*Why are we here? To create partnership. As fellow travelers on a common voyage, our purpose is clear. We can celebrate the opportunity to reclaim a quality of relationship that is the birthright of all people . . . Thank you for your courage, and bless you on your journey towards partnership in relationship.*

❧ Lew Epstein

*Chapter 15*

# A New Beginning

SO WHERE do we go from here? I hope that most of the answers to that question are already apparent. You can now understand why John Stuart Mill said, "When society requires to be rebuilt, there is no use in attempting to rebuild it on the old plan. No great improvements in the lot of mankind are possible, until a great change takes place in the fundamental constitution of their modes of thought."

I trust you can now understand the basic premise of this book: that we live in a particular paradigm, which is neither good nor bad. It just is what it is. But it has us be and act in a particular way. So *it*, not you or I or the people in your company, are responsible for our world being the way it is. The existing paradigm, the one right here and right now, is *not* set up to have a group of enthusiastic, confident, positive people working together on behalf of a future they have all committed themselves to. To the contrary, it is set up to have pettiness, gossiping, competition, conflict, arguments, and righteousness. You now understand why it is this way.

If we keep operating in the existing paradigm, we'll only get more of what we've got. So, as stated in the beginning of this book, it's necessary that we be clear about the existing paradigm and see it for what it is and how it has us be as human beings. Our discussion thus far has made it apparent why our companies, indeed our world, are in the shape they are in.

But here's the wonderful and liberating reality: the way we are as human beings is only one possible way of being a human being. We have already begun to propose an alternative paradigm, a paradigm designed to have cooperation, caring, cohesiveness, trust, respect, and most important, satisfaction, fulfillment, harmony, creativity, and productivity.

Once we commit to this alternative way of being, everything can begin to flow smoothly. Set up the field in the shape of a diamond, add bases and a pitcher's mound, and it's easy to play baseball. The only thing left to do is practice the new way of being until you get good at it, and that can be an exciting and enlivening experience if you're willing to commit yourself to it.

## The Importance of Commitment

As you move forward, a critical step is to find out who is on your team and who isn't. In personal relationships as well as in business, people often hang out waiting to see how things are going to turn out before they commit. They say, "I'll try out this relationship, this job, whatever, and I'll see how it goes. If it works out, or at least looks like it will work out, then I'll commit."

Unfortunately, this way of being almost guarantees that it's *not* going to work out. What makes things work out is being committed to them working out. Remember the law of cause and effect. If you are waiting to see how it turns out, what you produce is more waiting to see how it turns out.

So if you want it to turn out, commit! Remember our definition of a successful enterprise? It's a group of people working together on behalf of a future they have all *committed themselves to!* Does this guarantee things will work out? Unfortunately no, because there are a lot of other factors to consider. But it does stack the odds in your favor.

At the end of our retreats, we ask each person, "Are you willing to commit yourself to working with this group of people to design and create a future that you are all aligned with? No holding back; no waiting any more to see how it turns out? Are you willing to close the back door, put both feet in instead of one foot out and one foot in, and be willing to do whatever it takes to produce the result you all align on?"

You might think that's a lot to ask of anyone. But what's remarkable is that in the space created by empting the files, people almost always enthusiastically say yes. And with that yes, we have opened the door to an enormous new possibility.

## Stand Taking

Before we complete the discussion of the new paradigm, we have one more topic to discuss.

In the ordinary course of events, we are constantly making decisions about one thing or another. You could say that your job, more than anything else, is to make decisions. That's both good news and bad news about being the leader. It's good because you are the one who ultimately gets to make the decisions. It's bad because the process is often challenging and difficult, fraught with uncertainty.

So let's look at the decision-making process. Where do you normally look or what do you check in with when you have to make a decision? As with everything else we've discussed in this book, don't look for "the answer;" inquire into this.

Let me suggest one possibility. It's not the "truth;" it's just something to consider. Consider that you first determine what you think about the situation you are dealing with, and then you determine how you feel about the situation. But where do these thoughts and feelings come from? I suggest they come from your experiences to date. And when in time did those experiences occur? In the past. So when we look to our thoughts and feelings in our decision-making process, the future often resembles some version of the past.

This explains why so many people never change the events in their lives. They keep doing the same thing over and over again because they keep living their lives out of the thoughts and feelings they've created in the past.

The question is: "Is their another way?" Is there something you and I have access to so that we can create a future that, while honoring the past, is not an extension of the past? Absolutely!

We have a mouth and we have the ability to open that mouth and speak into existence a future that is not otherwise going to occur. That's called *taking a stand!*

As Max Weber, the German philosopher once said:

> I am under the impression that in nine out of ten cases I deal with windbags who do not fully realize what they take upon themselves, but who intoxicate themselves with romantic sensations. From a human point of view this is not

very interesting to me, nor does it move me profoundly. However, it is immensely moving when a mature man – no matter whether old or young in years – is aware of a responsibility for the consequences of his conduct and really feels such a responsibility with heart and soul. He then acts by following the ethic of responsibility and somewhere he reaches the point where he says: 'Here I stand; I can do no other.' That is something genuinely human and moving. And every one of us who is not spiritually dead must realize the possibility of finding himself at some time in that position.

History abounds with examples of the course of human events being changed because a person or a group followed the ethic of responsibility, as Max Weber defined it, and took a stand for some new course of action or possibility. The United States of America was created when our forefathers got together and declared their independence. Mahatma Gandhi changed the course of history when he took a stand for a free India. Martin Luther King, Jr. changed the awareness of people in the United States and launched the civil rights movement with his famous speech on the steps of the Lincoln Memorial. President John F. Kennedy launched the race to the moon when he took a stand for the possibility of landing a man on the moon and returning him safely.

Stand taking has tremendous power. As a leader in the new paradigm, you will always have to make decisions. But the question in the future will be: "Where will you look to find your answers?" Will you look to your thoughts and feelings, or will you look someplace else, such as to your commitments, your vision, your mission, your intentions, or your goals? We'll look further at this as we discuss designing the future of your company.

For now, I want to point out what may already be obvious. Taking a stand is risky business. Look at what happened to President Lincoln, Gandhi, Martin Luther King, Jr., and our forefathers. The first three got killed, and our forefathers had a war on their hands.

But while taking a stand is risky business, it's what distinguishes the ordinary leader from the extraordinary leader. Being willing to take stands is what ultimately will make you powerful and effective.

*Chapter 16*

# A New Paradigm of Being Human

IN THE previous chapters, I've painted what looks like a bleak picture of the current paradigm and the typical conversation in which we live. But if you look below the surface, you'll see just how true this picture really is.

Fortunately, another way of being human exists, and it's a way that doesn't come with such a high price tag. In fact, this alternative paradigm of being human encourages and supports people to become leaders who empower others and make the organization they lead one worth being a part of. And it's only this way of being that will allow you to make work truly work.

In designing our new way of being, the most obvious question is: "What is this human being's conversation going to be in regards to him or herself?" The new conversation is "I'm okay!" Why? Because being willing to take a stand for the most fundamental thing you can stand for – your own worth and value – is a critical step. As discussed in Chapter 11, as long as you're critical of yourself, you'll be critical with others. That's just the way it is. To reach your full potential as a leader, you must first commit to resolving the issues you have with you! And it starts with taking responsibility for the conversation you have about you, eliminating the "not okay" conversation, and generating a conversation that you are, indeed, okay!

The second question regarding our alternative paradigm is: "What is the conversation going to be about in terms of where there is to go?" The answer: No place! There is no place to go or get to. This is it. We're here. We've already made it. We always have made it. We have nothing to prove. We simply can't prove what has always been the truth. As Marianne Williamson so beautifully said: "We are brilliant, gorgeous, talented and fabulous. We are the children of God. We were born to make manifest the glory of God that is within us. It's not just in some of us; it's in everyone. And as we let our own light shine, we unconsciously give other people permission to do the same. As we are liberated from our own fears, our presence automatically liberates others."

Next, "Who is this conscious human being going to be interested in?" Other people! Once people handle themselves, once people realize that they are okay and that there's no place to go or get to, they naturally turn their attention to others. This was, for me, probably one of the most profound realizations that occurred as a result of doing the work this book discusses.

It's clear to me, in hindsight, that I spent most of my life with my attention on *me*, concerned with *my* survival, trying to get for *me* what I thought would make *me* happy. And, it never worked. For the most part, I was unhappy because no matter what I got, it was never enough. And what I didn't notice, until one of my coaches graphically pointed it out to me, is that I left a long list of hurt, angry, dis-empowered people in my wake.

But once I "handled" me, got that I was OK, and started putting my attention on what I could do for others, life, true life, began. I have never experienced, trying to do for me, the joy and satisfaction I receive seeing what I can do for another. This is one of the great paradoxes of life: As long as you're in life for what's in it for you, there's nothing in it for you. It's only when you are in life on behalf of what you can do for another that all of life's riches become available to you.

Finally, "What is this conscious human being going to be up to?" Lots of things, such as having fun; identifying talents, abilities, and interests; and figuring out a way he or she can use those talents, abilities, and interests to contribute in some way to others and life on our planet.

Every human being has something unique to offer, some gift to give, some contribution to make. When we stop the effort and struggle of "trying to make it" and when we stop being concerned with our survival, we become free to pursue our gifts. When we learn to come from trust and abundance, we stop doing things just to make a living and start pursuing what we are passionate about.

This is as good a time as any to ask yourself: "Are you doing what you're doing because you're passionate about it, or is it a job, something you fell into, something you're doing because you make good money doing it?"

## The Path to My Passion

In the 1990s I worked almost exclusively with lawyers and law firms. I can't begin to tell you how many lawyers I spoke to who admitted they were lawyers only because they didn't know what else to do with their lives, and it seemed like a way to make a good living.

I spoke to many others who were in touch with their gift and who knew what they were passionate about, but they were afraid to leave their law practice because they didn't think they could make enough money doing what they really wanted to do.

If you want to be a new paradigm leader, don't be like those lawyers. You won't win, and the people around you won't win either. Here's an important and almost unknown reality: you earn a specific amount of money not because of what you do, but because of where you have evolved to on the scarcity/abundance continuum.

In other words, you "make money" not with your labor, but with your mind. And you take your mindset with you wherever you go. So if you are making $200,000 doing one job, and you quit that job to pursue something you are more passionate about, it won't take long before you are again making $200,000, or more!

This is exactly what happened to me when I retired from practicing law to pursue my new career as a business coach. I had recently joined a large law firm and was two months away from being made a partner when I decided to retire. I was earning more money than I had ever made before. As a practical matter, I couldn't just walk out the door because I had many clients and lots of responsibilities. I was even managing one of the firms' branch offices.

So I made a deal with the firm to phase out over a year. During that year, I turned over my cases and my clients to another lawyer, and gradually I disconnected from the firm.

In the meantime, I began to pursue what was next, never really knowing what that would be. I was looking to discover my gift and see where and how to make it available.

This leads me to another belief of mine. That is, whenever you commit yourself to something, you are naturally and systematically led in the right direction. W.H. Murray, from The Scottish Himalayan Expedition summed this belief up best when he said:

> Until one is committed, there is hesitancy, the chance to draw back, always ineffectiveness. Concerning all acts of initiative (and creation), there is one elementary truth, the ignorance of which kills ideas and splendid plans: that the moment one definitely commits oneself, then Providence moves too. All sorts of things occur to help one that would never otherwise have occurred. A whole stream of events issues from the decision, raising in one's favor all manner of unforeseen incidents and meetings and material assistance, which no man could have dreamed would have come his way. I have learned a deep respect for one of Goethe's couplets: *Whatever you can do, or dream you can, begin it. Boldness has genius, power, and magic in it.*

The day I finally walked out of my law office for good, I still had no idea where I was heading. But an almost magical series of events occurred, none of which I could have imagined or planned. And while I did indeed go thirteen months without any income, I was led to the perfect job with the perfect company. Soon I was making more money than I ever did as a lawyer, even though I had neither the formal education nor training to be able to pursue my new profession.

## Your Next Step

Continuing with our new design, our conscious human being generates his listening and uses language to create the most empowering and inspiring picture for himself and everyone around him. He generates satisfaction and happiness in his conversation and looks for the gold in everyone he meets.

He neither complains nor gossips, but rather takes action whenever something is not the way he would have it be. He practices "The serenity prayer," popularized by Alcoholics Anonymous:

> God, grant me the serenity to accept the things I cannot change, the courage to change the things I can, and the wisdom to know the difference.

Our conscious human being does not withhold her communications, no matter how risky it seems to communicate. Rather, she takes responsibility for her upsets and disappointments and communicates everything appropriately and in a timely manner. Furthermore, when others communicate to her, she listens with compassion, takes responsibility, apologizes, and always forgives.

Sound like a daunting task? It is. At least it has been for me. But, it's all straightforward and simple, though not necessarily easy. Is it worth taking on? Absolutely! Is it worth committing yourself and your company to creating an environment where people get to be conscious human beings supporting each other in that endeavor? Absolutely!

## An Example

Remember the company that did development, construction, management, and leasing, where it seemed like everyone was making everyone else wrong? I went to the company's office and interviewed everyone. After completing the interviews, I had one of my more interesting conversations with the company president, Mike.

"I have good news and bad news," I began the conversation. "The good news is that I have identified the problem. The bad news is that it's you. These people are suffering because they need some leadership; they are looking to you to provide it, and you're not interested. You're mostly gone, doing your development thing, hoping things will turn out. Well they are not turning out. You're also not very good at acknowledging people and letting them know where they stand with you, and some of them are feeling insecure. And you can be negative and sarcastic. You constantly say things that are discouraging."

You can only imagine how you would feel if someone said that to you. But Mike was great. He didn't resist what I said at all. In fact, he knew it was the truth. So I continued, "People need a leader. Either you're willing to step up and be the leader, or we'll have to get someone else. But finding a leader is essential to moving forward."

After a slight pause Mike said, "I'd actually like to take it on. It might be fun. Can you coach me on being the leader?"

"If you're willing, absolutely," I said.

And so the journey began. First, we took the nine senior executives away for a three-day retreat, talked about everything we've discussed in this book, emptied the files, and completed the past. They all committed to work together to create a future they would all be satisfied with. We distinguished the new paradigm of being human, and they all committed to supporting each other in the commitment to become conscious human beings. Then it was time for them to get back to work.

The results were immediate, remarkable, and often amazing.

People outside the company frequently complained about one of the women on the team (we'll call her Laura), and when others received the complaints, they often agreed with the complainer. The first week back, someone complained about Laura to one of the men on the team who mistrusted her most. But instead of agreeing with the complainer, he defended Laura and took responsibility for the person's complaint. When I asked him why he did that, he responded that it was time to rehabilitate Laura's reputation in the community, given the commitment she had made.

The team continued its pattern of meeting on a regular basis, and the president started consciously acknowledging them for their efforts and accomplishments. But even more significant, when he would make a sarcastic remark, someone would immediately speak up and tell him to stop. It wasn't long before he did.

I continued to speak to the president on a weekly basis, coaching him on how to most effectively handle difficult situations, and I periodically checked in with different team members to see how they and he were doing. Within four months, they were working as a finely tuned machine, enthusiastically supporting each other and keeping their files empty. They all reported that the president was doing a great job as the leader. By the end of six months, my work with the company was done. The president was doing great, the team members were doing great, and the company was doing great.

Six months. That's all it took. Admittedly, it was a company of only ninety people. The bigger the company, the longer the process will take, but not proportionately. Once the team at the top starts working together in the new paradigm that we have discussed, things quickly start changing throughout the organization. More than two years later, the new paradigm is stronger than ever. Work can work!

*There is nothing more difficult to take in hand, more perilous to conduct, or more uncertain in its success, than to take the lead in the introduction of a new order of things.*

❧ Inscription from Machiavelli's tomb

## Chapter 17

# A New Paradigm of Being Related

IN ADDITION to our new paradigm for being a human being, which focuses primarily on how we will be and who people will be for us, we also need to design a new paradigm of relating to each other. Lew Epstein used to say that the highest form of human interaction is a "partnership." I've come to believe that a partnership is the only truly satisfying form of interaction. To the degree that people don't operate with each other as "partners" is the degree to which their relationships will be less than satisfactory. So let's discuss what I mean by a "partnership" relationship.

A true partnership relationship is a phenomenon in human interaction. Partnership, when viewed in this manner, provides a context for everyday living and for all of our relationships. If we don't nurture and care for the relationship, it will inevitably die. It is this failure to nurture our relationships that causes the breakup of countless companies every year.

If businesses are to succeed and endure, they must account for the human beings that are bound together in them. A true partnership relationship must include the following elements:

## ꙮ A Shared Vision

Relationships are a shared journey into the future, where each participant contributes what he or she has to offer to the partnership and receives the benefit of what the partnership creates. When people don't think of relationships in this manner, upsets are inevitable.

Recall my definition of a successful enterprise, which is a group of people working together on behalf of a future they have all committed themselves to. For this to be the case, the parties to the relationship need to understand the future or vision they share. Knowing this would go a long way to ending the bickering that seems so commonplace in personal relationships.

In a business context, a shared vision is frequently missing. It is my suspicion that if you randomly walk into most companies and ask the employees, "What's the company's vision?" the most common answer will be "to make money." And if you ask them, "To make money for whom?" the answer will likely be "for the owners, of course."

Now that wouldn't be a bad thing if making money for somebody else motivated people, but the reality is that it doesn't. So having an inspiring vision that people share is critical to creating a partnership relationship.

When I do the kinds of retreats discussed throughout this book, I always like to make sure people have time to create a shared vision. So not only do people leave the retreat feeling good about themselves and each other, they also leave with a sense of the future they are going to work together to create. This sense of an exciting future helps to keep people focused on staying in the new paradigm we have created, as they know staying there will be essential to having the shared vision become a reality.

## ❧ Inclusion

We live in a very individualistic culture. Our country is the birthplace of the entrepreneur. We are the "rugged individualists." Our folk heroes are John Wayne, the Lone Ranger, Amelia Earhart and now Superman, Batman, and Spiderman.

Entrepreneurs, in particular, are individual decision makers. If something needs to be done, they make a decision and do it. Could others be adversely affected by the decision? Yes, but the entrepreneur will deal with them later. Right now, someone has to make a decision.

Our entrepreneurial, bottom-line quality is both our strength and our weakness. It works to produce results, but it often doesn't work to build solid and deep relationships, and that's what's missing.

A true partnership operates in a way that is clearly distinct. Its people do not make decisions that affect others without fully discussing the decision with them. When an issue needs resolution, those committed to partnership work to build consensus. They listen to and consider every point of view. They make every possible attempt to reach a conclusion that works for everyone, with no one left out. They always consider other people's feelings and strong points of view.

The above discussion does not preclude the possibility of creating a management team or individual and delegating decision-making authority to that team or individual. But in such cases, the team or individual must be keenly sensitive to the individual points of view of the others with whom they work. When they need to make a decision, and there is doubt as to whether the decision will be acceptable to all, they must discuss all points of view to ensure a favorable outcome to all. In summary, in a true partnership relationship, decision makers are sensitive to the fact that they are not islands, that their actions impact everyone, and that everyone else's point of view is as important as their own.

This element of partnership is often the biggest source of complaints that I hear from people in companies when I begin a project. "They don't ask me my opinion," "I don't know what's going on," "Some of the things 'they' decide make no sense to me, but do you think 'they' ask me how I feel" are all too frequent comments I hear. Needless to say, these comments are not coming from turned on, motivated, highly productive employees.

Now I can hear what you are thinking: "This is going to take time. I can't go around and get everyone's opinion and build consensus. I'm too busy to do that." Yes, it will often take time. But do it anyway. You will save much more time in the long run not having to deal with people's upsets because they were not included. And you certainly will not have to deal with people attempting to sabotage your plans because they feel left out and unappreciated.

## Trust

In the ordinary course of events, people simply do not trust one another. Every child learns early in life: do not take candy from a stranger; do not talk to strangers; be careful! It is part of our culture to distrust others. So trust becomes something we give carefully. And to make matters worse, everyone has been taken advantage of, fooled, or duped on a number of occasions.

We believe that trust must be earned after a long period of careful scrutiny. Only after people have performed consistently, for an extended period of time, can we trust them, and only so long as they continue to perform. If they stumble, we quickly revoke that trust.

The problem with relating to trust in this manner is that it does not take into consideration the fundamental nature of human beings. The fact is that people are not trustworthy. People are fallible; that is part of being human. No one will consistently perform as promised, keep their word, and do everything they say they will do by when they say they will do it.

This being the case, we can relate to trust in another, more powerful way. We can generate trust by declaration, and stand for it on an ongoing basis. (Remember our discussion about taking a stand.) This is the kind of trust that is essential in a true partnership relationship. People agree to trust one another simply because it is the company's spoken commitment, while fully acknowledging that human beings will make mistakes.

When individuals do make a mistake, others can expect that they will acknowledge the mistake and do everything necessary to resolve it. Once resolved, an individual's humanness, or the fact that he or she has messed up, must not cause a revocation of trust. In this scenario, trust is a context for people to work together. It is something generated on an ongoing basis and a place to come from in dealing with the realities of business.

## ஃ Listening to Each Other

As discussed in Chapters 10 and 13, we need to listen *for the gold* and *with compassion*. This sometimes means listening for *possibility* or listening for the other's *commitment*. Whenever possible, it also means listening *and/both* and *win/win*.

When people are upset, it means getting their communication, not getting defensive and always apologizing. In this manner, people can feel safe with each other and true cooperation can result.

## ஃ Respect for Each Other

Respect is very much like trust. In the ordinary course of events, people earn respect after they have proven their talent and their ability to produce results. Often it's worse than that. People are frequently respected only because they are liked. If an individual is disliked, he or she is discounted and distrusted. This way of dealing with respect is dis-empowering in a relationship.

So again, in a true partnership it is essential that we generate respect by declaration and stand for it on an ongoing basis. Respect means acknowledging human beings and standing for their worthiness and value. Respect means giving up the right to judge and deciding to give respect based upon commitment rather than upon the results produced. Thus, an individual's humanness and seeming lack of productivity and perfection will not cause a revocation of respect. In this scenario, respect is a context for people to work together. It is something that is generated – a place to come from.

## ❧ Open and Honest Communication

As discussed in Chapter 13, open and honest communication involves keeping your files empty, taking responsibility for whatever you are experiencing, and talking about everything, openly, honestly and fully.

It also means talking only to the people who are the subjects of whatever communication needs to take place. No complaining about the person and no gossiping to another.

## ❧ Compassion for Each Other's Feelings

Recently, a few specific, psychological conversations have become fashionable. The terms "co-dependency" and "dysfunctional family" are on everyone's lips, and people rush to the store to buy John Bradshaw's latest book on healing the inner child.

We need to finally acknowledge that to some degree everyone is co-dependent and that all individuals come from families that were in some way dysfunctional. In fact, the entire world is dysfunctional. Crime, poverty, drug abuse, war, anger, and violence are everywhere. So within everyone is a sensitive, damaged, and often angry child who grew up in a world where appropriate vehicles to heal the hurts were unavailable. The simple phenomenon of growing up has left people damaged and feeling "not okay."

Despite all of the knowledge available today, appropriate means for dealing with this damage are still not within most people's grasp. So they bring the damage to work and act out in a number of unacceptable and inappropriate ways. People at work neither understand what is going on with an upset individual, nor do they know what to do about inappropriate behavior. We believe we can do little to help, and that it is an individual's responsibility to work out his or her own "stuff," single-handedly or with an appropriate professional.

There is, however, something we can do in the office. Faced with another's upset, co-workers can generate compassion, can take the time to listen, can try to understand and appreciate how it must be for the upset individual. Anyone can authentically care that another human being is hurt and upset. A little compassion goes a long, long way to having another feel he or she is not alone in life and that someone else understands and appreciates what he or she is going through.

## ⁑ No Competition

People at work would do well to model their relationships after sports teams, such as professional basketball or football teams. For example, on a football team, everyone plays a different position. Everyone has a different job, and the success of the entire team depends upon everyone doing his job, contributing what he has to contribute.

If basketball players compete with their teammates to gain individual recognition, there is little possibility of the team achieving its goals. Before the Chicago Bulls won their first NBA Championship in the 1990s, Michael Jordon beautifully said,

> It's hard to celebrate individual accolades with the team and with people, with fans. It's a lot better when you do it as a team, when you become champions as a team. Then everyone can feel some of the excitement that you feel.

And Karl Malone of the Utah Jazz said, in May 1998, after beating the LA Lakers in four straight games in the conference finals,

> When you put your minds together as a team, you can accomplish a lot of great things.

Most people do not see the parallel of teamwork in a company. In a company, people competing against one another appears healthy. It isn't. For one person to win, another must lose, and nobody likes losing. When people in a business compete with one another, the process of the partnership's disintegration begins. In a true partnership relationship, everyone understands his or her role and does the very best for the common good. In a true partnership relationship, people win and lose together.

Companies that have large sales staffs often do something that violates this rule with very negative consequences. They have contests and programs that pit each salesperson against the other and then they give awards, prizes, trips, and the like to the one or those who win the contest or produce the greatest result.

Imagine an end-of-year meeting with 50 salespeople where the grand "prize" is given to the top performer. The other 49 applaud politely, trying to be happy for the "winner," but are they really? At the end of the meeting, the reality is that there is one winner and 49 losers.

What about setting up a program where everyone competes against him or herself. Rather than trying to beat the rest of the team, each person's goal for the year is to increase *his or her* performance by some percentage over what *he or she* did the previous year.

Imagine this same group of people at this company's end-of-year meeting. What if 10, 20, 30 or however many people get some bonus, some prize, because they performed at a new level, compared to what *they* did before? In such an environment, people are encouraged to support each other, to work together, because now, in doing so, everyone can win! To me this is so obviously more desirable that I'm amazed that companies still have sales competitions that encourage people to sabotage their fellow employees.

## ❧ No Righteousness

It we were to take life and turn it into a board game, and if the board game could be set up to operate exactly the way human beings operate, then my candidate for the perfect name for the game would be "Be Right." Being right is the greatest human passion. People will do anything to be right. This need for people to be right shows up every day in every courtroom. It shows up in relationships, between groups of people, between nations, and between political groups. It's everywhere, and it's pervasive.

Not only are individuals *oriented* towards being right, they are also *committed* to being right. Unfortunately, when a person is committed to being right, that person leaves others who have been made wrong in his or her wake. This is why being right and being happy cannot co-exist. It may look as if being right provides happiness, but look again. The happiness is momentary. People are made wrong, relationships are destroyed, and employees fight with each other. In this right/wrong scenario, a partnership relationship is not possible.

A true partnership relationship operates in a clearly distinct way. Team members are willing to give up their positions, their opinions, their firmly held beliefs, and their need to be right in order to reach consensus, to serve the majority, and to discover what would work best for the whole. They listen to and consider every point of view. They make every possible attempt to reach a consensus, with nobody left out. People are more committed to the company's success than to their own passionately held positions.

## ♣ Embracing the Differences

Continuing with the sports analogy, not everyone can be a great quarterback, a great shooting guard, or a great shortstop. A football team has room for blockers and tacklers, running backs and receivers. Furthermore, every great quarterback knows that he is nothing without his supporting cast. Sports forces people to recognize and appreciate the differences in their teammates and to include those differences if the team is going to be successful.

Unfortunately, most people have not learned this essential lesson. Most people are constantly comparing others to themselves. They criticize others whenever they don't live up to some set of standards, or they envy them when they've exceeded them. This way of being fosters the right/wrong, good/bad phenomenon discussed previously, leading to envy, jealousy, and antagonism, the forerunners of the disintegration of most relationships.

A workable company has finders, grinders, minders, and binders. Finders bring in the work; grinders do the work; minders manage the company; and binders bring people together. Unfortunately, in our culture, we give more credit to a finder than to the others. But what's the good of finding without those to grind, mind, and bind?

In a true partnership relationship, everyone acknowledges and appreciates other people's contribution and uses each others' talents for the maximum benefit of the team. In a true partnership relationship, it is important that all involved recognize and learn to appreciate who they are and who their teammates are, and to include the differences rather than being irritated by them. When this is done, the differences can provide strength and opportunity to the company.

Does this sound like an exciting way to design our relationships? Yes. And while it sounds simple and straightforward, it's not so easy to do in practice. But like everything else we've discussed, it is worth taking on. I invite you to do so. You won't be sorry.

*Chapter 18*

# Aligning on a Vision

WE'RE ON the home stretch. We've distinguished the existing paradigm of being human and being related and designed a new, workable, empowering, and inspiring paradigm of being human and being related. Returning to our definition of a successful organization, which is a group of enthusiastic, confident, positive people working together on behalf of a future they have all committed themselves to, you can see that the tools for creating the first part of that definition are now clear. The last step is to create a future that everyone can be committed to.

After 18 years of working with organizations, I have developed a template – a series of questions – that when people are willing to confront, discuss, and resolve, they attain clarity as to the future the company is committed to. Here are the questions:

### ✦ What Are The Facts Now?

Here the objective is to get clear about what is true right now. Who are you? What does your company look like? Where is it located? What does it do? How many people does it have and serve? What does it look like physically? What are its products or services? Who are its customers? What are its revenues and profits? Write down all the details. Paint a picture of what people would see and what they would find if they walked into your company today. Stick to the facts.

### What Are Your Strengths?

What do you consider your strengths to be? What contributes to the company's success? What do you do well? What are the nice things people say about you? What do you want to maximize?

### What Are Your Weaknesses?

What do you consider your weaknesses to be? What gets in the way of the company's success? What could you do better? What are the things people, both internally and externally, complain about? What do you want to minimize?

### What Are Your Concerns; What Issues Are You Dealing With?

What do you worry about at night? What doesn't seem to ever get resolved? What is standing in the way of your success? What areas do not seem to be working?

## ❧ What Is Your Company Vision?

What's your vision for the future? If you had a magic wand and could create anything, what would your company look and feel like? If there were no limitations, if you could steer your company into the future and have anything and everything your heart desired, what would it look like when that happened?

Most companies have, at best, a set of goals and objectives. While it is important for a business to identify its objectives, vision is distinct from a set of objectives. Vision lies in an entirely different realm. It has to do with the nature and kind of business you want to create, the tone and feel of the business for all stakeholders. A vision is inspiring, as in "to land a man on the moon and return him safely" or "to develop a reputation in an industry for providing the highest quality products and the best customer service." A vision is the view of the future that the company is committed to creating. Vision serves to bind people together, as the Declaration of Independence did for our forefathers or as Lee Iacocca's vision for the future did for the employees of Chrysler.

In order to create a company's vision, you must answer several questions:

- What are the fundamental commitments in building this company?
- How would the owners or executives want the company to be so that they could be truly proud of it, happy, and excited about walking into it every morning?
- What are the company's commitments with regard to its customers?

- How would management want their customers to speak about the company? What about the employees?
- How does management want the employees to feel about working at the company?
- How would the owners or executives want to be treated?
- What is the company committed to with regard to the community in which it operates?
- What difference does the company want to make in the lives of its customers, its employees, and its community?
- What is the unique contribution that the company has to make?

Do these questions sound beyond the realm of ordinary conversation? They probably are but shouldn't be. They are the exact questions that are missing in so many companies, yet they need to take place if an inspiring vision is to emerge.

### What Business Are You In?

This is a basic question. In the days before airplanes, the railroads thought they were in the railroad business. So when air travel came along, they didn't get involved. Yet, had they seen themselves as being in the transportation business, a very different result may have occurred. So this is an important question. Exactly what business are you in?

I worked with a group of partners in a firm that took many weeks and many hours of discussion to answer this one question. They knew what business they *had been in*, but they were committed to using that information to advise rather than limit their discussion of what business they would be in in the future.

### ❧ What Products or Services Do You Offer?

Do you want to be all things to all people, or are you limited to a particular set of products and/or services? Successful companies are clear about the products and/or services they offer, and they stick to what they are good at. They have a recognizable brand that people acknowledge and relate to with trust.

### ❧ To Whom Do You Offer Your Products or Services?

Many successful companies were built because they had a clear picture of their customer. *USA Today* was written for a specific reader. Nordstrom's department store was designed for a specific customer. Now, many people other than the target market read *USA Today* and shop in Nordstrom's, but both continue to focus on their target customer.

Focus is critical for successful marketing. If you're not clear about whom you are targeting with your products or services, it's like shooting an arrow into a fog and hoping you will hit the bulls-eye.

### ❧ What Is Your Price?

Are you going to compete based on price or on the value you create? Nordstrom's clearly doesn't try to be the cheapest in its field. In fact, it may be more expensive than its competitors. But many people are willing to pay more given the service they receive. As a coach, I always prided myself on charging *more*, not less, than my competitors. My attitude was that if you wanted the best, and wanted real results, then you'd stop whining about the price and make an investment in your future. If you want to shop for the cheapest, you'll have to go someplace else, but don't complain if you don't get the results you want.

## ᴥ What Is Your Purpose/Mission?

As discussed previously, a powerful mission and an inspiring vision for its future are essential to a company's success. They serve as a source of inspiration for the employees, unleashing their creativity, productivity, and effectiveness. Without such a mission and vision for the future, their work quickly becomes exactly that – work – a dull routine that saps people of their natural aliveness and motivation and leaves them dis-empowered and resigned.

Although it may have many other names, the mission of an organization is embodied in what is often referred to as its "purpose" or "mission" statement. For example, one of the most successful American companies of our time, Johnson & Johnson, is studied in almost every major MBA program in this country, particularly for its "Credo." Johnson & Johnson's "Credo" is acknowledged throughout its organization as the primary reason for the company's success. As do all well thought-out mission statements, the Johnson & Johnson Credo sets forth the company's fundamental principles and values, and these principles and values will typically include a number of elements.

The first element essential to a clearly stated and effective mission statement responds to the question "What do we do?" The second element addresses the question "What are we committed to in doing what we do?" The third element considers the question "Who are we for our customers or clients?" The fourth element defines "Who are we for our employees/staff?" The fifth element seeks to answer "Who are we for our owners?" And finally, the sixth element is responsive to "Who are we for our community?"

In the case of Johnson & Johnson, the company's key executives consider it their primary purpose to keep the Credo and what it represents in front of every single employee, all of the time. At Johnson & Johnson, the Credo is not merely a collection of noble words. It is something that lives and breathes within every person in the organization.

So what might a mission statement look like? Here is the Johnson & Johnson Credo:

We believe our first responsibility is to the doctors, nurses and patients,
to mothers and all others who use our products and services.
In meeting their needs everything we do must be of high quality.
We must constantly strive to reduce our costs
in order to maintain reasonable prices.
Customers' orders must be serviced promptly and accurately.
Our suppliers and distributors must have an opportunity
to make a fair profit.

We are responsible to our employees,
the men and women who work with us throughout the world.
Everyone must be considered as an individual.
We must respect their dignity and recognize their merit.
They must have a sense of security in their jobs.
Compensation must be fair and adequate,
and working conditions clean, orderly and safe.
Employees must feel free to make suggestions and complaints.
There must be equal opportunity for employment, development
and advancement for those qualified.
We must provide competent management,
and their actions must be just and ethical.

We are responsible to the communities in which we live and work
and to the world community as well.
We must be good citizens – support good works and charities
and bear our fair share of taxes.
We must encourage civic improvements and better health and education.
We must maintain in good order
the property we are privileged to use,
protecting the environment and natural resources.

Our final responsibility is to our stockholders.
Business must make a sound profit.
We must experiment with new ideas.
Research must be carried on, innovative programs developed
and mistakes paid for.
New equipment must be purchased, new facilities provided
and new products launched.
Reserves must be created to provide for adverse times.
When we operate according to these principles,
the stockholders should realize a fair return.

*Johnson & Johnson*

Long, but impressive.

On a simpler note, the following is an example taken from the real estate development company discussed earlier in Chapter 13:

We are a real estate solutions company. We use our extensive knowledge and experience to provide development, construction, property management, leasing, and/or consulting services to our customers to enable them to maximize the value of their real estate investments.

We know real estate because we own real estate. We listen and present a process that is well thought-out and strategic.

We are reliable and trustworthy and act with a high degree of integrity, consistent with our commitment to always exceed the expectations of our customers.

We are a company our employees are proud of. We provide them a fun, exciting, challenging and team-oriented work environment, where they want to come and participate, which encourages and provides opportunities for them to grow personally, professionally and spiritually, and where they are recognized and rewarded for their accomplishments and contributions.

We are committed to maximizing the return on the investment for our customers and owners, that our customers receive value, and that our employees realize their financial goals so that everyone wins out of their participation with our company.

We are good corporate citizens. We give of our time, resources and expertise to worthwhile community organizations; we encourage our employees to participate in community and family activities of their choice and we support them in such activities.

It's immediately apparent that this mission statement includes the six elements discussed previously. Paragraph one sets forth what the company does. Paragraph two sets forth what the company is committed to in doing what it does.

While paragraphs one and two are obviously related, paragraph two sets forth the company's fundamental commitments to its clients. Here the firm commits itself to "listening" and presenting processes that are "well thought-out" and "strategic." They are "reliable," "trustworthy," and operate with "integrity." Its commitment is to always "exceed the expectations of their customers." With the quoted words, the company's mission begins to emerge.

Paragraph three sets forth the company's commitment to its employees. The company is not interested in just any kind of work environment, but only a fun, exciting, challenging, and team-oriented work environment, where the employees want to come and participate. It is also clear about the type of opportunities the company is committed to providing its employees.

Paragraph four contains an all-important commitment to the company's ownership. This is a critical element to any organization's purpose, for without profitability, the organization's other objectives will not be fulfilled.

Finally, paragraph five sets forth the firm's commitment to its community. Note that it is up to the employees to identify the areas in which they seek to give back to the community.

If viewed simply as a hollow group of well-intentioned words on a piece of paper, such a mission statement might provoke disdain and skepticism. If the words, even with good intention, were placed on a piece of paper and tucked neatly in a drawer, the document would be worthy of such an attitude.

On the other hand, if the words represent management's deeply felt commitment, if the document is presented to the employees as the company's underlying philosophy, and if the executives and employees alike work together to fulfill the mission, such a written statement will serve as a source of inspiration for the employees, unleashing their creativity, productivity, and effectiveness. Such a mission statement can achieve for a company the same motivational effect as Johnson & Johnson's famous Credo, and a company can enjoy the same long-term benefits that such an inspired environment provides.

### ❧ What Is Your Strategic Vision?

Remember the first question, "What's so?" Now it's time to project five or more years into the future and create a "what's so" for then. Given the strengths, the weaknesses, the vision, the products and/or services, if I walk into the company in five or more years, what will it look like? This becomes the picture that everything is driven towards.

### ❧ What Are Your Key Objectives For The Next Year?

Now it's time to create three to five key objectives for the next year which, when accomplished, will launch the company powerfully in the direction of its strategic vision. In other words, we're working backwards. Start with the overall vision. From that, create a five-year strategic vision, and then work back to what needs to happen in the next year so that the strategic vision becomes a reality. From this, you can further create objectives for the next quarter, the next month, the next week, and the next day. The key is to work backward from the big picture and the future.

### ❧ What Is Your Culture?

If the mission, company vision, strategic vision, and key objectives set forth the company's philosophy and direction, the culture establishes the "rules of the road." Every company has a culture. Usually, the culture just evolves over time. I recommend that you create a culture as an expression of the organization's commitment to the new paradigm discussed herein.

The organization's culture establishes what behavior is acceptable and expected and what is not. It covers how people are expected to act individually, with each other, with the company's customers and vendors, and with the community in general. A well thought-out culture statement goes a long way toward creating a conscious paradigm. Here's the culture statement created by the real estate development company, whose purpose statement appears earlier in this chapter:

**Who we are as a company:**

- We are here to serve our customers.
- We recognize and appreciate the uniqueness of each individual and the importance of everyone's contribution to the company. We seek to utilize each person's unique strengths and abilities. No one person is more important than any other.
- We provide all employees opportunities to grow, develop and advance professionally.
- We encourage people to take the initiative to keep up with the industry and their own personal growth and development.
- We maintain a clean, well-organized, comfortable environment. While our atmosphere is casual, dress is appropriate to a professional business environment.
- People's commitments to their moral and/or religious values are never sacrificed.

## Who we are as individuals:

- We are our word. We are committed to keeping the promises we make. When we cannot keep our promises, we communicate responsibly.
- We are self-starters; we take initiative and freely and willingly perform our duties at or above the level expected of us.
- While at work, our focus is on the business of the company and we manage our personal lives so that they do not interfere with this focus.
- We are proud of the company and loyal to it.
- We are goal oriented and goal driven. We are accountable for the results we commit to producing.
- We enjoy our work, have a positive attitude, and bring fun and enthusiasm to whatever we do.
- We know what work is expected of us and we get our work done completely and on time. We always do the best job we possibly can.
- We do not need the presence of owners, managers, or supervisors for the fulfillment of our accountabilities.
- We are punctual in attendance and always deliver a full day's work.
- We're willing to do whatever it takes to get the job done, including being available for overtime when the need arises.
- When our work is completed, we actively look to assist our co-workers.
- We are committed to maximizing efficiency by delegating wherever possible and appropriate.

- We advance in the company by improved performance of duties and by the acceptance of increased responsibilities.
- We are always seeking to increase our knowledge and improve our skills to better enable us to perform our responsibilities.
- We promptly acknowledge our mistakes when they are recognized and immediately act to correct them.
- We do not discuss our pay or benefits with others in the company.
- Our job titles describe job functions and not status.
- We share in the financial and other successes of the company.
- We experience satisfaction and fulfillment out of the company's accomplishments and the benefits derived by the company's customers.
- We use appropriate language in the work environment.
- We do not sabotage the goals or purposes of the company by pursuing an inconsistent personal agenda.
- We are dynamic and talented; we are focused, highly productive, and we constantly raise the bar.

## Who we are with each other:

- We always communicate openly, honestly, directly, and in a timely manner with each other and with our customers. We do not withhold our communications. We are discreet and appropriate when we communicate.
- We do not complain or gossip about each other, the company, or our customers. Rather, we express our

dissatisfactions and suggestions for improvements and only to someone who can do something about it.

* We operate as a team; operation is seamless to the customer.

* We support each other and take initiative to solve all problems, whether created by us or not.

* We treat each other fairly and with dignity and respect and acknowledge the value of everyone else's work. We do not belittle or abuse other people.

* We care about each other. We treat each other with compassion.

* Our work environment is high energy and fun.

* We rely on each team member to be a key contributor to the objectives of the company; to be responsible and accountable for the commitments they make; and to share their ideas, knowledge, techniques, and expertise with the others.

* When we become aware of information relating to a customer, a sale, or any other aspect of our business, we promptly share such information with all who have a need to know or will be impacted by the information.

* We are a team; we win or lose together.

* We are sensitive to and responsible for the consequences our actions have on others.

* We value comments and suggestions from all those with whom we work. We express gratitude and appreciation to our co-workers for their efforts.

* We encourage and support others in the company in their pursuit of worthwhile causes and their personal aspirations.

## Who we are with our customers and the community:

- We treat everyone we meet as a customer. "Customers" include architects, engineers, vendors, brokers, tenants, and everyone else we deal with in doing our jobs.
- We recognize that how we conduct ourselves in the community reflects on the reputation of the company and we are responsible for our conduct.
- We greet every customer with a smile.
- Every contact with a customer is designed to leave them feeling favorably impressed with the level of service they receive.
- We treat our customers as part of the family.
- We talk straight with our customers and proactively seek to ensure that they are not misled.
- We maintain our professional image in our dealings with customers on the telephone and in person. We promptly respond to telephone calls, e-mails, and correspondence.
- We are creative in our thinking about our customer's needs and look for creative solutions to solve their problems. We're willing to do whatever it takes to make sure the customers' needs are satisfied.
- We honor and respect the confidences of our customers and all matters involving the company.
- We seek opportunities to be actively engaged in good causes and encourage our fellow workers to do the same. The company is willing to financially support employees in community service projects and, whenever possible, we participate as a group in worthwhile community causes.

### ❧ What Is Your Organizational Structure?

The final step in designing the future is to create an organizational structure that will take you there. Most companies do this by putting all of the people in the organization on a piece of paper and then organizing them in some logical and manageable way. Or, they organize the company based on how it exists today. Both approaches only keep the company stuck where it is.

Here's a better approach. Look at your five-year strategic vision. Consider that it has been fulfilled. Now, imagine that none of the people presently in the company are there in five years. Create an organizational structure to efficiently and effectively manage the company as it will be then; no names, just use boxes, functions, and titles. Design the most workable management structure you can imagine for that company.

When that's done, and only when that's done, put the people you presently have into the boxes. You will immediately see what's presently missing in your organization and what will be necessary when you achieve your strategic vision. You will become clear about what will have to happen over the next five years. So pencil in some dates as to when each of the vacant positions will be filled.

When you follow this approach, the organizational structure becomes a road map to fulfilling the strategic vision, and it pulls you into the future you've always known was possible.

*This is the true joy in life, the being used for a purpose recognized by yourself as a mighty one; the being a force of nature instead of a feverish selfish little clod of ailments and grievances complaining that the world will not devote itself to making you happy. I am of the opinion that my life belongs to the whole community and as long as I live it is my privilege to do for it whatever I can. I want to be thoroughly used up when I die, for the harder I work the more I live. I rejoice in life for its own sake. Life is no "brief candle" to me. It is a sort of splendid torch which I have got hold of for the moment, and I want to make it burn as brightly as possible before handing it on to future generations.*

⚜ George Bernard Shaw

*Chapter 19*

# Conclusion

WE'VE COME to the end of this journey, but your new journey towards becoming a leader and a participant in the new paradigm is just beginning.

Looking back over my years of experience, I am convinced that the majority of human beings *do* want life to work and want to participate in making work work. I can honestly say that I haven't met even one mean-spirited, truly nasty person among the thousands I've worked with. Yes, I've met a few with some really rough edges, but they all ended up being like the Los Angeles lawyer who got angry all of the time. They had a legitimate commitment but a lousy strategy for fulfilling it. And when shown the error of their ways, they were willing to change their strategy and become part of the solution, not the problem.

For you, that is good news. Why? Because no matter how bad it may seem in your organization, what is unquestionably true is that the majority of people want it to work and will be your ally in making that happen.

So now it's up to you. You are standing on the doorstep of an incredible opportunity. What you have read is a process I have done dozens of times with remarkable success. All that has been missing in the past were the insights and tools necessary to shift people from the paradigm we inherited to the paradigm that's possible.

What's your choice? At one extreme, you can have found this information interesting, possibly enlightening, and maybe even extraordinary. But if you leave it at that and don't act on it, I suggest that slowly but surely, the information will fade away – not because that's what you want, but because the "pull" of the existing paradigm is so strong that it's like a rip tide, constantly pulling you under. It's like fishing for crabs. If you have a big basket and put a crab in it, it will crawl out and escape. But if you put several crabs in the basket and one tries to escape, the others will pull it back in.

So go to the other extreme and take a stand for a new possibility! Commit yourself to a course of action that will allow you to create the paradigm you now know is possible. Draw a line in the sand. Gather your key team members and enroll them in this course of action. And, most important, create a structure to support you in moving forward.

### Take a Stand for Commitment and Support

Most resolutions for change don't work because they are nothing more than good ideas. There is no commitment, and even when there is, there is no structure of support. For example, suppose you decide to start jogging three days per week. You are excited and you want to do it, but you never have jogged before.

Your first step is to get a pair of running shoes, shorts, a water bottle, etc. Armed with the right equipment, you decide that tomorrow at 5:30 a.m. will be your first attempt at jogging.

You go to sleep the night before ready for the task. But then what happens? The alarm goes off at 5:15 a.m. and you are confronted with how dark it is, how cold it is to get out of bed, and how much you really want to sleep more. Suddenly, jogging doesn't seem like such a good idea. So you turn off the alarm and go back to sleep. You had no structure of support.

If you really want to start jogging, I would suggest that you find someone who regularly gets up at 5:15 a.m. three days a week, and who commits to making sure you do what you say you will do. He calls you at 5:15 a.m., tells you to get your butt out of bed, and arrives at your home in fifteen minutes to take you running. You agree with him in advance that he will not take no for an answer and that he'll drag you out of bed if necessary so that you keep your commitment. Most important, you build in consequences if you don't keep up your end of the deal.

I once had a partner who kept coming late to our partnership meetings. I told him one day that his tardiness was unacceptable and that there had to be consequences if he continued with this behavior. So he agreed, on his own, to pay me $1 for every minute he was late for a meeting. The first meeting he was late by five minutes and paid me $5. The next meeting he was late by seven minutes and paid $7. I was beginning to hope he would continue being late. But when he was twenty minutes late to the next meeting and had to pay me $20, he was never late again. Consequences work!

You, your team, and your company have an enormous opportunity here. You can break out of the ordinary, out of business as usual, and create an extraordinary organization. And now you have the guide. I invite you to take a stand, commit, get into action, and build a structure of support. Ask yourself, "What kind of paradigm do I want to create?" Remember that whatever you want *is* within your reach, but don't expect anyone to simply hand it to you. Only you can make it happen.

Is such a shift simple? Yes. Is it easy? No. But like the real estate company, the San Francisco law firm, and the dozens of other companies that have exerted the effort and committed themselves to this approach, it can all become a reality.

As you move forward with this new commitment, I wish you the best on your journey. And if by chance you should stumble or fall, remember that you can always come back and revisit the conversation here, re-commit, get re-inspired, and start again. As you have likely heard so many times before, "life is a journey, not a destination." So enjoy the trip, have fun, and always remember, it's just a conversation.

# Index

For information about our
coaching, retreats, programs, seminars or workshops,
contact

THE HUNTER PARTNERSHIP ALLIANCE
Irvine, California
Toll free: 877-237-0207 • Phone: 714-573-8855
Fax: 714-573-8860
Visit our company web site: www.thpalliance.com
Or send us an e-mail: info@thpalliance.com

For information about booking
Scott Hunter as a speaker
Call the numbers above
Or visit our web site: www.makingworkwork.com
Or send Scott an e-mail: Scott@makingworkwork.com

Free on the web
• Articles on Teamwork, Relationship, Communication
• Self-Assessment Questionnaire

Sign up for our free monthly Electronic Newsletter
The Coach's Corner
Sign up information is on both of the above web sites

Hunter Alliance Press

# About the Author

For more than 17 years, Scott Hunter has been the go-to expert for hundreds of companies committed to creating relationships that will take them wherever they want to go. He inspires individuals, transforms organizations, and achieves bottom-line results for his clients. Business leaders turn to Scott when they are looking for breathroughs in enthusiasm, productivity, and profitability.

A graduate of The City University of New York and The George Washington University School of Law, Scott has been an entrepreneur and business owner for over 35 years. He was also an adjunct professor at Western State University College of Law, where he taught courses on the principles of business and personal success.

Since the late 1970s, Scott has been researching what it takes for people to produce extraordinary results in their personal lives and careers. Through his studies, Scott realized that relationship is the key to accomplishment and just about everything else a person wants in life. Until people know how to create meaningful, quality relationships, they cannot fully achieve their goals, *including their business goals.*

This insight led Scott to apply what he learned about relationships to his work in the business arena. In the last 12 years, Scott has conducted over 100 corporate retreats for groups as small as 2 and as large as 44, consistently producing breakthroughs in the participants' relationships with each other. This has predictably produced dramatic shifts in the company's level of accomplishment.

As a consultant and coach, he has worked with over 150 corporate clients in working arrangements lasting just a weekend to as long as 10 years. As a speaker, Scott has delivered over 1,000 speeches. He delivers his customized presentations with poignant stories and anecdotes that allow participants to clearly see themselves in his message. He has the uncanny ability to cut to the chase, uncover the truth, and leave people in action, in their lives and in their businesses.